Michael Paraskos is an art historian and writer. Previous books include *In Search of Sixpence* (2016) and *Barfrestone* (2024), and he has written for numerous periodicals, including *The Guardian, Spectator* and *Sculpture Journal*. He has also appeared on radio and television in Britain, Cyprus and Sweden, and is editor of the journal *Pygmalion*.

He is a Senior Teaching Fellow at Imperial College London, where he lectures on art history, and visiting lecturer at the City and Guilds of London Art School. He is an Honorary Professor in Art History at York St John University and a Fellow of the Royal Society of Arts.

ISBN: 978-1-7384987-2-7

Published by the Orage Press
16A Heaton Road
Mitcham
Surrey
CR4 2BU
England

© MMXXVI All rights reserved. No part of this publication may be reproduced, performed, distributed, or transmitted in any form or by any means, including photocopying, recording, or other electronic or mechanical methods, without the prior written permission of the publisher, except as permitted by law. Michael Paraskos has asserted his right under the Copyright, Designs and Patents Act 1988 to be identified as the author of this work.

Stass Paraskos, Στας Παράσκος and Cyprus College of Art are registered trademarks used by permission of the trademark owners.

Front cover: detail of the Great Wall of Lempa, Cyprus — ©2026 Estate of Stass Paraskos.

Stass Paraskos:
Critical Frameworks

*For my mother
Mary*

Introduction

There is a story that a government official in Cyprus, visiting *The Great Wall of Lempa* in 2025, made a joke about the artist who created it, Stass Paraskos, having worked in a fish and chip shop in his youth. A poor joke of course, and doubly so as Paraskos never worked in a fish and chip shop. The amusement of the bureaucrat in thinking he did may say less about Paraskos than it does about the enduring class prejudices of the social elite of Cyprus. More importantly in the context of this study, it tells a tale about stories being told designed to deliberately diminish a person's standing.

This book is about those stories. Or, we might say, it is about the different ways in which tales are established and perpetuated. To turn our language into something more academic in tone, we might say it is a book about how particular narrative structures, or plots, are established when discussing an artist like Paraskos, to present him in a particular way, often at odds with reality. In other words, the stories told about Paraskos and other artists are not necessarily the truth — and perhaps the real truth is a false and unattainable goal in any case — they are biased and partial stories. In some cases this is an inadvertent bias, but as the case of the story told by the Cypriot civil servant shows, it can also be deliberate bias intended to diminish and marginalise.

I would like to say that Paraskos is now seen as one of the most significant artists to emerge from Cyprus in the twentieth century and that position is without doubt. But his elevation to that status was by no means certain, and in the continuing ambivalence towards him in both government circles and amongst the official guardians of art on the island, that status remains precarious. As we shall see, that precariousness was evident throughout Paraskos's life, as he faced a constant misunderstanding of his art and a diminishment of his achievements. That this continues after his death is puzzling, and so what I want to suggest through this book is that we put aside any clichés we might have about the life and work of Paraskos, and revisit his art with fresh eyes that might get us closer to the truth about his remarkable vision and achievement.

I should perhaps say *what I think was his remarkable vision and achievement* as I cannot claim this text is the unadorned truth about Paraskos, only that it is

my approach to him. I have my biases too. But in my
approach I have tried to rethink Paraskos outside of the
clichés we might have about him, such as the idea he
represented an essential Cypriotness in his art, or that
he was a naïve artist, or that he was in any sense an
apolitical painter. Using a modified version of the
theory of emplotment, as theorised by Hayden White, I
have attempted to approach the various readings of
Paraskos and his work as narrative plot devices, which
have both intentionally and unintentionally placed him
in a constraining framework that has had the effect of
diminishing his achievement. The frameworks, or
'plots', applied to Paraskos have frequently marginalised
him by presenting a narrative understanding of his
work that is at best partial, and at worst totally
misleading. In following this approach I have
augmented White's working of emplotment theory so
that it encompasses more overtly political
understandings of art, to mitigate the sometimes
frustrating denial in White of what seem like the
obvious political connotations of his ideas. The most
pressing of these is that emplotment can seem in White
to be a neutral affair, as though everyone is in some way

free to define and assert a narrative reading with equal authority. This seems patently untenable, and while I cannot find evidence of White actively asserting some kind of Nirvana-like world in which we all have equal power, similarly I cannot see him recognising that some narrative frameworks or plots have more social reach than others simply because of who is asserting them.

This is particularly important when looking at Paraskos, whose artistic career effectively began with an assertion by British art critics that he was some kind of innocent *fou sacré*. Even when meant admiringly, this label emplotted a reading of Paraskos that misrepresented the sophistication of how he understood his work, and repeatedly marginalised him from the mainstream art world. It also annoyed him and led to him making repeated assertions that it was not true. That these assertions appear to have gone unheard is effective testimony that the power to emplot a narrative is not equally distributed.

Consequently, White's emplotment theory has only been a starting point, and it has been necessary for me to augment it with reference to other cultural theorists, particularly those engaged in exploring post-colonial theory. It seems to me that it is almost impossible to really explore the art of Paraskos without also going into colonialism as he was born in a British colony, migrated to Britain because of the policies of the British colonial government and, crucially, even when he returned to Cyprus experienced what Homi Bhabha has called the mimicry of the colonial mindset by the newly-installed social and political elite in independent nations like Cyprus. Aligning this with White's theory of emplotment leads to a suggestion that the British colonialist framework that tied Paraskos into a plot of naïvety, innocence and some kind of folklorish Cypriotness, was maintained by both the government officials and, later in his life, by the art world in Cyprus. In effect, rather than challenging and rejecting a Western colonial mindset employed by the British while ruling Cyprus, and also evident in the attitude of Britain to its Cypriot migrant population, the emergent Cypriot elite that took over running Cyprus in 1960, and which is still in place today, appears to have internalised that mindset. This is evident even if the rhetoric of the Cypriot ruling elite claims otherwise, so that they have become mimics of the Western colonialists they replaced, not only in their actions but in their world view.

How this has manifested itself is fairly consistent and has created a curious parallel between how the post-independent Cypriot elite and the former colonial power of Britain has viewed Paraskos. At its best it has seen Paraskos as being some kind of naïve Cypriot, a self-taught artist who celebrated Cypriot village life in his art. At its worst it has presented him as a Zorba character, relishing any opportunity to undermine and dupe those in authority. As we shall see this was particularly evident in discussion of Paraskos while he was in Britain in the 1960s and 70s. The art critic of *The Guardian* newspaper, Merete Bates, described Paraskos as 'still a sunny peasant at heart even in the grimy brick-work of suburban Leeds.'[1] At the same time another art critic, W. E. Johnson, writing in *The Northern Echo*, suggested Paraskos had managed to dupe the eminent writer Herbert Read into thinking he was a clever artist.[2]

---

[1] Merete Bates 'Stass Paraskos' in *The Guardian*, 22 May 1970, 8
[2] W.E. Johnson, 'A Second Look at Paraskos' in *The Northern Echo*, 22 May 1970, 7

As this indicates, Paraskos was seen by some British critics as being an artist who is naïve, innocent, backward and also scheming, duplicitous and tricksy. These are tropes often found in British colonial depictions of subject peoples, but in the case of Paraskos it was not inevitable. Also writing for *The Guardian* newspaper, M.G. McNay recognised that the primitivist framework was not appropriate to Paraskos. 'Primitive is the last tag you can hang on Stass Paraskos.' The lines he drew might look child-like, McNay noted, but Paraskos 'knows what the business end of a brush is.'[3]

That the line of argument found in Bates and Johnson was also adopted later by Cypriot critics is shown in Eleni Nikita's 2015 essay on modern Cypriot art in which Paraskos was described as having 'adopted an unsophisticated and naïve artistic vocabulary.'[4] This was despite Paraskos being adamant on numerous occasions that it was wrong to read his work in this way.

---

[3] M.G. McNay, 'Stations Paraskos Exhibition' in *The Guardian*, 7 May 1966, 6
[4] Eleni Nikita, 'The Visual Arts: An Overview' in Miltos Miltiadou et al. (eds.), *Window on Cyprus* (Nicosia: Press and Information Office, 2015) 229

In a 2013 interview with Christina Lambrou, Paraskos stated:

> How can someone who taught at a university level for thirty years be naïve? I taught at almost every college in England. Well, I can't be that naïve, can I? The way I work is the way that suits me. It's personal, but it's not naïve.[5]

One of the arguable consequences of emplotting Paraskos in this way is that, with the emergence of more conceptual art in Cyprus in the 1990s, his work came to be perceived by later artists and critics in the newly developed university art departments and contemporary art spaces as belonging to an earlier, less intellectual phase of Cypriot art. That phase was seen as having been superseded in the dominant art institutions by more theory-oriented art. In effect, he became the peasant artist Bates had framed him as being, and someone regarded, at least in

---

[5] Χριστίνα Λάμπρου "Συνέντευξη στη Στας Παράσκος' in *Politis*, 28 October 2013. Online version https://www.parathyro.politis.com.cy/features/interviews/145584/parathyro.politis.com.cy

the eyes of the newly emergent university lecturers and gallery curators of Cyprus, as incapable of being read through an intellectual lens that might pass muster with the Western art world to which they aspired. This echoes the class-inflected discomfort that sometimes characterises institutional responses to artists perceived as culturally or socially peripheral to normative Western conceptions of contemporary art.

I do not present this idea as a statement of fact, or even of my own belief. Rather it is a possibility that I explore in this book through reference to recent critical theory in art, literature and post-colonial studies. In this I hope to establish the point of this book, which is to present different ways of approaching Paraskos and his work which do not fall back on the clichés of the past, and especially not on suggestions that are, in some cases, patently untrue. Paraskos could never be a naïve artist as he attended art school in England, and was taught there by some of the most important figures in the development of radical post-war art pedagogy in Europe. This included figures like Harry Thubron, Tom Hudson and Maurice de Sausmarez with global reputations in the history of art education. Indeed,

Leeds College of Art in this period was described by the artist and art critic, Patrick Heron, as 'the most influential in Europe since the Bauhaus.'[6] Paraskos even went on to teach at Leeds College of Art, where he became good friends with notable figures in the development of performance art, including Robin Page. Page was a key figure in the Destruction in Art Symposium held in London in 1966, the same year he joined Fluxus. While Paraskos never engaged in Happenings or Performance Art himself, these were the intellectual circles he participated in, which remove him far from the legitimate use of the label naïve. With this in mind, I explore in this book the possibility that we need to rethink two under-examined aspects of Paraskos's work, his writings and the structure known as the Great Wall of Lempa. With his writing, I have focussed on a diary he kept in 1968, recording a visit to Cyprus in the company of the Leeds-based poet Martin Bell, in which Paraskos wrote on the seemingly impossible task of arranging a meeting with the President of Cyprus, Archbishop Makarios, in order to get his help in establishing the Cyprus College of Art.

[6] *The Guardian,* 12 October 1971, 49

With the Great Wall of Lempa, a sculpture wall that surrounded and partly-filled the yard of the former Cyprus College of Art premises in the village of Lempa, I explore the possibility of re-conceptualising it as a quasi-performance, or at least heavily conceptual installation piece, redolent of the issues raised by Page and others in both Fluxus and the Destruction in Art Symposium. When looked at from this perspective we face the possibility of seeing the diary, Great Wall and even the Cyprus College of Art itself, as a single work of art, spanning a period of almost 50 years.

    The idea of an art school being a work of art in itself is, of course, an extraordinarily radical idea. Indeed this was recognised in 2006 when the Manifesta Organisation decided to stage the sixth version of its peripatetic art biennial in Cyprus, proposing to frame the event as an art-school-as-work-of-art. The stated aim of this was to localise the event and disrupt the discourses that pitted the centre against the peripheries in Western culture. As I explore in chapter six, the problem with the approach of Manifesta was that they seem to have assumed Cyprus was a *tabula rasa* when it came to contemporary art practice, and immediately discounted any evidence that might have suggested Paraskos was already doing much of what they proposed at the Cyprus College of Art in Lempa. In this we can again see how the emplotment of Paraskos as a naïve artist led to a misreading of both him and his work. While a more nuanced reading of Paraskos could have made him a natural ally of the Manifesta project, by applying the very Western neo-colonial gaze they claimed to want to undermine Manifesta saw in Paraskos an unintellectual artist, incapable of contributing anything to their stated mission. It is hard not to see this as resulting from an internalised neo-colonial mindset that elevated preconceived Western notions as to what a contemporary art space should look like to the detriment of seeing value in what already existed on the ground.

In exploring these themes I am mindful of the need to avoid the sense that Paraskos was a passive actor in the process of emplotment. To do so would be, I believe, to simply reinstate the same narrative structure of centre and periphery, in which the centre has agency and the periphery has none, that I am at pains to challenge. As we see from his time in England, where he seems to have actively distanced himself from any singular identity as a migrant, in order to establish an identity as an artist, Paraskos was very much capable of emplotting a framework for himself. Similarly, as we shall see through the use of literary theory, the act of writing a diary can itself be seen as an act of self-conscious emplotment, particularly in the context we see with Paraskos of using the diary form as a medium for art. By extending our understanding of the diary into a starting point for the Cyprus College of Art, and ultimately the Great Wall of Lempa, we can see it as a creative act of emplotment that indicates Paraskos was very much an actor with agency.

The aim in all of this is to approach the work of Paraskos from new and different angles. Through this we can benefit from the opportunity to gain new insights into his work and its social context, and equally importantly, insights into the means and motives of those who have, consciously or not, framed the narrative of Paraskos in ways that reflect institutional priorities at odds with his own.

Like the Great Wall of Lempa itself, this aim should not be seen as a finite project in which we look at what has happened, and try to correct what we consider to be the wrongheaded approaches of the past. Rather it should be seen as an ongoing project in which different approaches are considered and applied to build up an ever more complex understanding of Paraskos and his place in both the Cypriot and globalised art worlds. From that perspective there are no wrongheaded approaches, only a plurality of methods and meanings, not all of which will compliment or agree with each other, but which will develop into an understanding of Paraskos that goes beyond emplotting him as a peasant painter, a child like naïve or an unintellectual innocent.

Consequently, this book does not seek to define Stass Paraskos once and for all, but to undefine him, to show that the narratives surrounding his art are not truths but constructions, acts of emplotment shaped by the historical conditions that produced them. The aim is less about establishing a new canonical reading than attempting to reveal the mechanisms by which canons are made. To return to Paraskos after this, even if we think we know him, is not therefore, simply to revisit one artist, it is to engage a larger question about how artists are framed, read and remembered, and how those processes continue to shape what we are told counts as art, intellect and value.

It is my hope that what will emerge is not the final word on Paraskos but the opening of a conversation about how we look at artists from Cyprus, or indeed from any site considered peripheral to the Western canon. The argument developed here is specific, yet its implications are wide. If Paraskos was emplotted as naïve, folkloric or unschooled, it was because art history itself has too often operated through inherited binaries, such as centre and periphery, modern and traditional, intellect and instinct, male and female, coloniser and colonised. These categories have not simply described artistic production, they have ordered it, shaping who is seen, how they are valued and what is written about them. To challenge the frameworks that have limited our understanding of Paraskos is therefore to challenge the discipline as a whole.

Consequently, the study of Stass Paraskos sets down a marker for the writing of art history in Cyprus, and, by extension, in any postcolonial context. It calls for a genuinely postcolonial agenda, not merely the inclusion of previously marginalised figures into existing narratives, but the rethinking of the narratives themselves. Such a project requires the dismantling of the hierarchies inherited from colonial and other metropolitan art systems, and the establishment of new, pluralistic frameworks grounded in local experiences open to transnational dialogue. It involves cultivating a critical language that can speak of Cypriot art, and of any art produced outside dominant centres, without recourse to the familiar tropes of authenticity, folk identity or belated modernity. It demands self-awareness to recognise and challenge internalised discourses imposed from the outside.

Paraskos's life and work offers a testing ground for this agenda precisely because he does not fit easily into inherited categories. His art is at once local and international, modern and mythic, conceptual and sensual. His teaching at the Cyprus College of Art sought not to replicate Western academic models but to create an autonomous space for experimentation, a microcosm of what an alternative, decolonised art history in a decolonised art school in a decolonised nation might look like in practice. To engage seriously with Paraskos is therefore to engage with a model of artistic practice that anticipates the pluralism and critical reflexivity now demanded of global art history.

The next task, for scholars, artists and students alike, is to continue this work. That means returning to Paraskos's paintings, writings and teaching not as relics of a naïve past, but as provocations to think differently about the future, to re-examine Cypriot art not through imported frameworks but through its own material, mythic and historical conditions, and to connect those conditions with broader global movements in ways that resist assimilation into a single, Western, narrative. The goal is not to replace one canon with another, but to cultivate a field in which multiple perspectives can coexist and interact, in a dialogic rather than hierarchical art history.

If this book has one concluding argument, it is that the study of Paraskos is not a niche or regional pursuit. It is a case study in how art history might be remade, how it might move beyond the binaries that have structured it since its formation, toward a more open, plural and self-aware discipline. Paraskos's art, in its defiance of easy categorisation, invites precisely such a shift. To look at him anew is to glimpse the possibility of an art history that is no longer written from the centre outward, but from the margins inward, or better still, from everywhere at once.

A final, but important point to note regarding this book is that it is in my mind a companion piece to an earlier book I produced on Stass Paraskos, entitled *In Search of Sixpence*. Many of the themes in the two books are similar, for example the migrant experience in Britain and the centrality of the 1968 diary. But the forms are very different. Despite this, both books exist in my mind as twin art history texts, and ideally should be seen as complimentary pieces, like two leaves of a single diptych, together forming the whole work. Neither is intended to be definitive or the final word on their subjects, but each still represents a different approach to art history writing of equal validity.

If this book began with a small story told by a bureaucrat to diminish Paraskos, it ends by proposing that such stories, when re-examined, re-narrated and re-emplotted, can also restore him to the complex, critical and creative artist he always was.

Chapter 1:
The Red Woman:
landscape, myth and politics

It is always best to start with the art. After all, isn't that what this book is about, an artist and his art?

Perhaps. But as much as it is about an artist and his art, it is about how we talk about artists, and how we talk differently about different artists, conceptualising and labelling them along the way. It is about how the identity of an artist is not always in the hands of the artist, as other forces come into play, such as their gender, their perceived ethnicity, their place of birth, where they choose to spend their working life and so on.

This will become more apparent as we proceed, but let's start by trying to tie the question of identity to the actual works of art made by an artist, specifically the artist Stass Paraskos. In this opening chapter I want to explore a recurring motif in the paintings of Paraskos, namely the image of the red woman, and its significance to Paraskos's sense of identity.

As a motif, the red woman can be seen in works from the start of Paraskos's career, the earliest from the 1950s, through to the end of his life in 2014. Far from being a mere formal device, I want us to consider the red woman as being a possible nexus of identity in his art, a figure in which Cyprus is re-imagined as memory, myth and place. Through the lenses of Yi-Fu Tuan's topophilia and Gaston Bachelard's poetics of space, I want to look at the red woman as a poetic longing for home, a condensation of lived experience and the sense of *Sehnsucht* for that which is lost or one is in the process of losing. At the same time we will recognise that the red woman motif also engages with a longer tradition of feminising landscapes that, as critics from Carolyn Merchant to Gillian Rose have shown, risks re-inscribing patriarchal tropes of possession and control.

To begin, however, let's look at a different colourway, specifically the function of the green-skinned woman, called Siloën, in Herbert Read's 1935 novel *The Green Child*. In *The Green Child* Read describes the skin of Siloën as being:

> faint green shade, the colour of a duck's egg. It
> was, moreover, an unusually transparent
> tegument, and through its pallor the branches
> of her veins and arteries spread, not blue and
> scarlet, but vivid green and golden. The nails
> were pale blue, very like a blackbird's eggshell.[7]

At first glance the green skin of Siloën might seem an arbitrary conceit, a way for Read to display his modernist credentials by presenting her as though she were a living expressionist painting. But the device is in fact carefully chosen. While indebted to the visual idioms of modernism, it also recalls medieval traditions in which symbolic colour emblems signified the relationship between humankind and nature. In this respect, Siloën has a clear literary ancestor in the folk-legend of the green children of Woolpit, reported in twelfth-century Suffolk, and finds a broader resonance in mediaeval romance literature, most famously in *Sir Gawain and the Green Knight*. Just as Read's green woman fuses myth, folklore and modernist invention, I would like us to consider Paraskos's red woman as operating in

---

[7] Herbert Read, *The Green Child* (London: Robin Clark, 1935:1989) 25

a similar way, acting as a personification of the Cypriot earth, a figure in whom memory, myth and longing converge.

Although the red woman recurs in numerous works across Paraskos's career, let's focus on just two examples. The first is *Red Woman*, of 1972, which presents a female figure shown facing left, almost in full profile, seated against a background of horizontal bands of colour. These bands, green above, yellow in the middle and blue below, create an abstract, stratified field behind the figure, with the lowest blue band also resolving into the form of a chair on which the figure sits. The upper bands, green and yellow, are loosely brushed with shifting tonal variations, while the blue is flatter and defined by a thick black cloisonnist outline. At the left hand edge of the canvas there are two flat vertical stripes, one blue and the other green, which introduce a harder, graphic element into the painting that recalls the backdrops of Pauline Boty's Pop Art paintings.

The figure itself is painted in a rich Tyrian purple, a colour associated with Byzantine royalty, but here broken into rough patches of varying tone that enliven the body's surface. The figure's hair is a vivid green, tinged with yellow ochre and edged with a black contour. Paraskos's familiar monogram, *Stass*, is inscribed in the lower right corner in bold black letters. The composition as a whole is flat, consistent with modernist pictorial language, yet the body itself is modelled to suggest depth and rounded form. This tension between the hieroglyphic and the sculptural, or between the symbolic sign and the sensuous body, captures one of paradoxes at the heart of the red woman motif across Paraskos's work, its simultaneous materiality and other-worldliness.

The second painting is a much later work that employs a very different compositional language. *Red Nude*, painted in 1995, takes the form of a landscape painting, its surface articulated as a flattened patchwork of fields in vivid reds, yellows, and greens. In the upper left corner a small village anchors the background, while scattered across the composition are several human figures, while the nude of the title reclines horizontally across the foreground. In the middle distance, slightly to the left, stand two women, one dressed in red, the other in blue, their upright forms counterbalancing the recumbent nude, seemingly deep in conversation. At the extreme left hand edge, a more enigmatic presence appears, a hooded figure of indeterminate sex, resembling a kind of watcher, overlooking the scene, its hand resting on a curious striped bird that seems to act as its familiar.

As with the 1972 *Red Woman* the space is flat, but here that flatness is even more accentuated with little tonal variation between the foreground and background negating any real sense of recessional depth. Similarly, the human figures show little of the modelling seen in the earlier work.

The two decades that separate these paintings saw a significant shift in Paraskos's style, yet the connecting thread between them remains the presence of the red woman. This figure appears in several other canvases too, suggesting that it functioned as a symbolic motif for Paraskos within his oeuvre. The use of the human figure, particularly the female body, as allegory is of course nothing new. Almost every god or goddess of the Greek and Roman pantheon can be understood as an allegorical embodiment of abstract qualities, while later secular traditions produced equally resonant female personifications, from Britannia in Roman Britain to Marianne in post-Revolutionary France. These, however, are public and collective symbols and Paraskos's red woman does not appear to belong to this category of image.

Ernst Gombrich offers a useful framework here, distinguishing three modes of pictorial meaning: (1) straightforward representation; (2) shared public symbolism; and (3) private symbolism, the last of which may be consciously intended or emerge unconsciously.[8] His tripartite model recalls Erwin Panofsky's three levels of interpretation, pre-iconographical, iconographical, and iconological,[9] but Gombrich's intent was somewhat different. Panofsky's iconology sought to move beyond surface and conventional meanings to reveal the underlying symbolic values or mental habits of an age, whereas Gombrich warned that such readings risked engaging in excessive speculation unless grounded in demonstrable evidence.

---

[8] Ernst Gombrich, *Symbolic Images: Studies in the Art of the Renaissance* (London: Phaidon, 1972) 12

[9] Erwin Panofsky, *Studies in Iconology: Humanistic Themes in the Art of the Renaissance* (Oxford: Oxford University Press, 1939) 7-14

Applying Gombrich's more cautious criteria to Paraskos's red woman paintings, we clearly encounter the first mode of pictorial meaning in that we see the image of a woman, but the question is whether she also carries symbolic meanings, and if so, whether these should be read in terms of collective conventions or private significance known only to the artist. The absence of any established red woman figure in broader Cypriot culture, combined with Paraskos's silence on the subject, means the question cannot be definitively answered. Consequently the questions have to remain open as unproven possibilities, but we can speculate as to what the figure might mean.

As we can see in the 1972 painting, *Red Woman*, and other examples, such as *Another World* of 1966, Paraskos frequently gave his red women figures green hair. From a straightforward formalist perspective this corresponds to basic colour theory of the type Paraskos would have learned at Leeds College of Art, with red and green appearing as colour complementaries on the Goethean colour wheel. But from a Panofskian perspective this might relate to a wider symbolic structure expressing collective ideas of fertility, landscape and identity within Cypriot culture. In the eastern part of Cyprus in which Paraskos grew up the soil is often a rich red, called *terra rossa* or *kokkinoyis*, ideal for growing the famous Cyprus potatoes. If this is also the red of the red woman paintings, perhaps the green of her hair is the verdant growth that appears on this soil in winter and spring, or even the green rocks that also make up a significant part of the landscape of Cyprus, their colour coming from the copper ore they contain. If so, the symbolic meaning we are looking for could be construed as being either conscious or unconscious, and in both instances the red woman would operate as an allegorical representation of the land to which Paraskos was intimately connected in his youth. In saying this, however, we are engaging in speculation without textual or contextual evidence, meaning that such interpretations remain hypothetical. Following Gombrich's warning, we must acknowledge these are no more than possibilities and cannot be asserted as facts.

Yet a sense of connectedness to a specific earth recalls Herbert Read's own reflections on childhood and place. Like Paraskos, Read was the son of a farmer, he grew up in the rural North Riding of Yorkshire, and often wrote about the imprint of this early environment on his psychological makeup. In 1933 he produced a series of prose-poem vignettes, called *The Innocent Eye*, that recorded episodes from his childhood on the family farm. For Read, such experiences exemplified the formative role of what he called 'elementary sensations', the primal encounters with the world that become the foundation of later psychic life. He wrote:

> All life is an echo of our first sensations, and we build up our consciousness, our whole mental life, by variations and combinations of these elementary sensations.[10]

As Leena Kore Schröder has observed, this understanding of childhood fed directly into *The Green Child*.[11] The novel's protagonist, Oliver, is not simply a fictional surrogate for Read in a landscape reminiscent of Yorkshire, but an artistic doppelgänger, a figure

---

[10] Herbert Read, *The Innocent Eye* (London: Faber and Faber, 1933) 8
[11] Leena Kore-Schröder, 'Rumbling in the Depth: *The Green Child* and the Uncanny' in Michael Paraskos (ed.), *Re-reading Read: New Views on Herbert Read* (London: Freedom Press, 2007) 190

whose union with Siloën at the novel's close becomes a literal return to the earth that produced them both. Indeed, in a later reworking of *The Innocent Eye* entitled *The Contrary Experience*, Read described his own deep sense of rootedness in his childhood home as a feeling of being 'kin to the stone'.[12] Siloën, then, is more than a symbol of that relationship, she is its embodiment. Here we might recall Gombrich's discussion of 're-presentation' in which hyphen between 're' and 'presentation' is important. Unlike representation, which is grounded in likeness, or allegory, and operates as metaphor, re-presentation is equivalence, the prototype of the object depicted being presented again. As a result the artistic image becomes the double or doppelgänger of what it depicts. This mode of meaning resists easy rational analysis, veering instead into the terrain of anthropology and magical practice. As Gombrich notes, 'We know that in magical practice the image not only represents an enemy [but] may take his place ... We know that the fetish not only symbolises

---

[12] Herbert Read, *The Contrary Experience* (London: Faber and Faber, 1963) 291

fertility but has it.'[13] The image is thus, not a sign of power but the power itself.

Such a conception might not have been alien to Paraskos, whose earliest encounters with art came through the Orthodox Christian icons of his village church. In Orthodox Christian belief, the icon is not a representation of the saint depicted but a manifestation of the saint's presence, what Ernst Benz has described as 'a kind of window between the earthly and celestial worlds.'[14] To gaze at the Mother of God in an icon is not to see an image of the Virgin Mary, rather it is to see the Virgin Mary herself. As a result, the red woman need not be seen as a representation of a specific individual or a public allegorical figure, but as a re-presentation, an embodiment or doppelgänger, of the earth of Cyprus itself. Whether consciously intended or unconsciously generated, she may have functioned for Paraskos as the living image of the land that bore him.

If this appears too mystical a turn, perhaps it is useful to turn to Yi-Fu Tuan's distinction between *space*

---

[13] Ernst Gombrich, *Symbolic Images; Studies in the Art of the Renaissance* (London: Phaidon, 1972) 125

[14] Ernst Benz, *The Eastern Orthodox Church* (New York: Anchor Books, 1963) 6

and *place* to bring the whole concept down to earth. For Tuan, space is an open and abstract category, but through lived experience it becomes place, invested with memory, affect and identity.[15] This process of transformation is not only rational and physical, but imaginative and symbolic. The recurring red woman may be read as a personification of the earth of Cyprus, not as landscape in a literal sense, but as an embodiment of the artist's lived relationship with his homeland. In this sense, the red woman functions as what Tuan describes as the transformation of a mere space into a meaningful place, a nexus of memory, myth and affective attachment. Tuan writes: 'What begins as undifferentiated space becomes place as we get to know it better and endow it with value.'[16] This distinction between space and place finds an echo in the way the red woman seems to mark not a generalised human figure, or even a generic symbol of femininity, but a figure deeply tied to the Cypriot land. In her, we might speculate, Paraskos appears to crystallise the

---

[15] Yi-Fu Tuan, *Space and Place: The Perspective of Experience* (Minneapolis: University of Minnesota Press, 1977) 6
[16] *Ibid.*

transformation of Cyprus from a mere physical location, a space, into a place imbued with his own affective and bodily attachment.

Tuan's related notion of *topophilia*, namely the emotional bond between people and their environment also resonates closely with Paraskos's recurring motif of the red woman. As Tuan notes, 'Topophilia is the affective bond between people and place or setting. It differs greatly in intensity, subtlety, and mode of expression.'[17] For Paraskos, the red woman can be understood as an expression of such topophilia, embodying his childhood memories of the red soil of *kokkinoyis*, the seasonal greening of the landscape, and the copper-coloured rocks of the Troodos mountains. More than descriptive landscape painting, these works seem to reconfigure physical features of Cyprus into a humanised figure that carries the affective weight of longing, exile and erotic memory.

Equally important in all of this is the role of myth and narrative in Tuan's account of place-making. For Tuan, stories and cultural traditions 'thicken' space

---

[17] Yi-Fu Tuan, *Topophilia: A Study of Environmental Perceptions, Attitudes, and Values* (New York: Columbia University Press, 1974) 4

into place, embedding landscapes with symbolic resonance beyond their physical properties. In Cyprus, folklore is saturated with female presences, from the nymphs of springs to spirits haunting rivers and groves, to semi-legendary heroines like Arnaude de Rocas. Although not a representation of a specific myth, folkloric figure or female personification, Paraskos's red woman can still be seen in this light, at once personal and mythological, a private memory and a cultural archetype. She becomes what Tuan would call a 'field of care', a locus where memory, affection and myth converge to create meaningful attachment.[18]

Through this lens, the red woman does not simply illustrate Cyprus, she enacts it as its enixa, giving it life. Her red body is not only the colour of passion or danger, but of soil, blood and memory. Her presence in painting after painting suggests that for Paraskos the red woman was not merely a symbolic motif but a means of re-presenting the island itself as a lived and felt place. She becomes a *genius loci* in Tuan's phenomenological geography, the spirit of place given

---

[18] Yi-Fu Tuan, *Space and Place: The Perspective of Experience* (Minneapolis: University of Minnesota Press, 1977) 159

human form as a recurring figure through which Paraskos negotiated his own relationship with homeland, exile and belonging.

Despite my suggestion that Tuan brings us down to earth, there is, of course, a poetic dimension in Tuan's concept of topophilia which echoes the work of numerous other writers. Gaston Bachelard's *Poetics of Space*, in particular, seems relevant to Paraskos. For Bachelard, places are never neutral or objective, but are suffused with reverie, memory, and archetypal resonance:

> Space that has been seized upon by the imagination cannot remain indifferent space subject to the measures and estimates of the surveyor. It has been lived in … not in its positivity, but with all the partiality of the imagination.[19]

As with Read's claim that our earliest experiences of nature provide the foundation for later encounters,

---

[19] Gaston Bachelard, *The Poetics of Space*, trans. Maria Jolas (New York: Orion Press, 1964) xxxvi

Bachelard suggests that the poetic relationship to the *genius loci* of a particular place creates what we might call a poetic inscape, nurturing the imagination and ultimately feeding artistic creation. Bachelard writes: 'It is attached to a sort of expansion of being that life curbs and caution arrests, but which starts again when we are alone.'[20]

This sense of imaginative habitation resonates strongly with Paraskos's recurring motif of the red woman. The red woman does not function simply as a figure within a composition, or as a generic allegory, but as a condensation of Cyprus itself as lived and remembered. She resonates with Bachelard's notion of 'intimate immensity', which is the paradox whereby the most personal and enclosed of spaces open out onto the vastness of memory and imagination. This offers a way of understanding the red woman as both erotic body and expansive landscape. In her, Cyprus is not represented as a measurable territory, but as an interiorised, affective presence, shaped by the subjective partiality of memory and exile.

---

[20] Gaston Bachelard, *The Poetics of Space,* trans. Maria Jolas (New York: Orion Press, 1964) 183

Like Read, Bachelard also emphasises how childhood memories of place persist into adulthood, transfigured by reverie. In this respect, Paraskos's red woman can be read as a poetic homecoming, a figure in which the sensory impressions of the Cypriot soil, colour and light are preserved and transformed. Much as Bachelard's childhood home became for him a storehouse of memory and imagination, so too we can speculate that the red woman served as a psychic dwelling place for Paraskos, a figure through which he could continually revisit the intimate immensity of his homeland, even in exile.

In saying this, a note of caution is necessary. One of the potential problems with this kind of personification of the landscape is its immanent gendering. The land becomes female, earth a mother, nature a lover. This trope has deep roots in Cypriot culture itself, from prehistoric earth goddesses to the later Greek mythologies of Aphrodite, the native goddess of Cyprus, born from the sea. Paraskos was clearly aware of these traditions, as the author of *The Mythology of Cyprus*.[21] This feminised reading of Cyprus

---

[21] Stass Paraskos, *The Mythology of Cyprus* (London: Orage Press, 2016)

continued into the early modern period, when Venetian artists repeatedly personified the island as Venus after Venice's takeover of Cyprus in the fifteenth century. Most strikingly, on the façade of the Loggetta del Sansovino, facing St Mark's Basilica and the Doge's Palace in Venice, the sculptors Danese Cattaneo and Tiziano Aspetti carved Cyprus as Venus in the form of a reclining nude. Around the same time, Venetian painters such as Giorgione and Titian produced celebrated images of Venus that can also be read as allegories of the island. These examples reveal how easily the allegorical personification of land as woman becomes entangled with unequal power relations. Carolyn Merchant's work is helpful in understanding the way fifteenth-century rationalism transformed the way Western culture perceived nature, with Merchant arguing from an eco-feminist standpoint that with the rise of modern science, especially rationalist philosophy, nature came to be understood as something to be subjugated by superior force. This was increasingly expressed in gendered terms with nature needing to be controlled through possession, domination and penetration. Merchant is explicit in connecting these metaphors with parallel justifications for the subordination of women in early modern society, as philosophers such as Francis Bacon argued that the female earth was to be bound into service, her secrets squeezed from her and her womb forced to bear fruit.[22]

Represented as a female body, exposed to the male gaze, images of Aphrodite-Venus became signifiers of possession and control, and the political conquest of Cyprus was naturalised through the eroticised conquest of woman. More recently this concept has been taken up by the feminist writer on geography, Gillian Rose, who has critiqued the historic and continuing projection of patriarchal authority onto the landscape through linguistic metaphor. According to Rose: 'The masculine gaze constructs the feminine as nature: landscape as a feminine space which the masculine occupies, possesses, and controls.'[23]

Clearly Paraskos risks falling into this diegesis in depicting Cyprus as the red woman, and more especially as the red nude. But Rose's approach may

---

[22] Carolyn Merchant, *The Death of Nature: Women, Ecology, and the Scientific Revolution* (New York: Harper & Row, 1980), 171-72

[23] Gillian Rose, *Feminism and Geography: The Limits of Geographical Knowledge* (Minneapolis: University of Minnesota Press, 1993) 71

offer another interpretation of Paraskos's figure that in the end undermines this trope. The historic narrative labelling of Cyprus as a female figure that is ripe for subjugation and exploitation does not fit easily with Paraskos's representation of the red woman, and we know from his political outlook he would have been unlikely to accept this narrative structure. Even the nude of Paraskos's 1972 painting *Red Woman* is not the supine and accessible *Sleeping Venus* of Giorgione, nor the coquettish courtesan of male fantasy in Titian's *Venus of Urbino*. This is an upright woman, naked but seemingly as much in control of her nudity as Michelangelo's David is of his. Indeed, if we are to find historical analogies in art, the red woman of this painting more resembles Rodin's *Thinker*. If the placing of the left hands in both the Giorgione and Titian accentuate the accessibility of the pudendum, in the Paraskos the left hand seems to guard the figure's genitals, which are not, in any case, clearly visible to the viewer. If Giorgione and Titian, as well as Cattaneo and Aspetti, depict the female Cyprus as open and available to the male viewer's penetrating gaze, Paraskos's red woman in *Red Woman* is far less accommodating. Her presence resists easy consumption, and as a result she cannot be reduced to the passive territory of patriarchal allegory. Consequently she may suggest something closer to Gillian Rose's concept of *paradoxical space*, in which we encounter not a singular, heteronormative reading of the feminised land, but a proliferation of possible meanings that undermine the Enlightenment impulse to define, categorise and control through a singular male narrative.[24] Rather than resolving into one authoritative interpretation, *Red Woman* generates a field of ambiguity and contradiction.

In noting this, we encounter a rarely discussed aspect of Paraskos's work, its unambiguous political messaging. There is no doubt that Paraskos's art was often directly political. Works such as *Cypriot Women Raped by Turkish Soldiers* (1967), *Liberty Abandons Cyprus* (1972), *Massacre at Qana* (1992), and *The Murder of Kutlu Adalı* (1996) testify to an artist unafraid to comment on contemporary political events in stark, visual terms. It is also worth remembering here Paraskos's difficulty in

---

[24] Gillian Rose, *Feminism and Geography: The Limits of Geographical Knowledge* (Minneapolis: University of Minnesota Press, 1993) 155

being assimilated into the British art world of the 1960s. As Stuart Hall and Avtar Brah have both observed, the art of diasporic subjects could never conform to modernism's formalist neutrality. It was necessarily narrative, experiential and political, grounded in histories of struggle that Western institutions preferred to exclude.[25] For Paraskos this political engagement was reinforced by his frequent newspaper writings, and if we extend the idea to reappraise our understanding of Paraskos's depictions of Cypriot village life, including images of the red woman, these too can be read not simply as nostalgic reflections on a disappearing world, but as critical landscapes where human interactions and contemporary social tensions are laid bare.

The red woman in *The Red Nude* (1986) differs from *Red Woman* (1972) in that she appears cowed, perhaps beaten, while villagers loom in the background, led by two sinister black silhouettes in the middle ground. Perhaps what is brought to mind is the

---

[25] Stuart Hall, 'Cultural Identity and Diaspora,' in Jonathan Rutherford (ed.) *Identity: Community, Culture, Difference* (London: Lawrence & Wishart, 1990) 222–237; Avtar Brah, *Cartographies of Diaspora: Contesting Identities* (London: Routledge, 1996) 208–209

disturbing scene in Nikos Kazantakis's *Zorba the Greek* in which the young widow is stoned and stabbed outside the village church.[26] Only the artist, possibly a self-portrait, shares her space, hands in pockets, gazing with sadness at the vanquished figure at his feet. A similar sense of social judgment pervades Paraskos's painting *Disapproval* (1994), in which a semi-naked woman lies on a bed as black-clad village women look on in shock. The theme recurs again in *Whisperings* (1995), where two lovers in the background are subjected to mockery by villagers placed in the foreground, and in *Dishonoured* (1996), this time transposed to a modern city, where the grotesque crowd echo the jeering faces of Emil Nolde's *Mocking of Christ* (1909) or Edvard Munch's *Golgotha* (1900).

     Far from presenting willingly subjugated female nudes, these paintings depict female figures who remain resistant, their vulnerability charged with defiance. They provoke, rather than resolve, moral questions. Through them we are forced to choose sides, to identify with the mocking crowd, the helpless Zorba-like artist looking on, or the exposed, but unyielding, nude herself.

---

[26] Nikos Kazantakis, *Zorba the Greek* (London: Faber and Faber 1961) 262

In this way, Paraskos generates precisely the kind of paradoxical space described by Rose, and even something of Bracha Ettinger's matrixial space in which images that resist singular interpretation and instead open up a multiplicity of possible meanings about sexuality, power, violence and resistance, and most of all questions concerning the positioning of the gaze of the viewer.[27]

As we see here, there is a clear difference between the upright, even confident, depiction of the *Red Woman* of 1972 and the prostrate images that appear in the 1980s and 1990s. A transitional work is *Red Nude* (1986), in which the female figure is viewed as if from above, positioned on the left of the canvas, while on the right two shadowy male figures are locked in conversation. Their ambiguous presence suggests plotting or gossip, and lends a menacing undertone to the scene. Although the figure still recalls the 1972 *Red Woman* in her compositional prominence, here she appears more defensive, her hands drawing in to shield her body. Perhaps in this we see a composition that

---

[27] Griselda Pollock, 'Thinking the Feminine' in *Thinking the Feminine: Theory, Culture & Society* 2004 21:1, 5-65

begins to echo Artemisia Gentileschi's *Susanna and the Elders*, in which the female nude is exposed to the invasive scrutiny of male figures who threaten her autonomy. But what explains this change?

To answer that question perhaps we need to look at Cypriot society more broadly. Paraskos was in Cyprus during the traumatic events of 1974, when a coup d'état, orchestrated by the military junta ruling Greece, took place against the democratically-elected government of Cyprus. This triggered a Turkish military invasion and the subsequent division of the island. Despite the struggle against British colonial rule in the 1950s and the low-level civil war that continued to rage in the 1960s, it was the events of 1974 that most represented a break with the optimism of the past. It was the moment when the romanticised vision of Cyprus as an idyllic paradise seemed irrevocably broken. In the years that followed, as money and speculative development came to dominate public life, trends Paraskos vocally opposed in his newspaper articles, the island itself, and its people, could appear to have been beaten, corrupted and under constant threat. It might be argued that the later depictions of the red woman embody precisely this altered vision of Cyprus, no longer confident and assured, but exposed, harassed and vulnerable to violation.

    The red woman in Paraskos's work is neither a simple allegory, nor a purely formal device. She emerges instead as a richly layered figure at the intersection of myth, memory and politics. From her earliest appearances in the confident upright nudes of the 1960s and 1970s to the more vulnerable and threatened figures of the 1980s and 1990s, she gathers into herself the imprint of Paraskos's lived experience and of Cyprus's turbulent modern history as he understood it. Read through Yi-Fu Tuan, she is the condensation of Cyprus as *place*, transformed from abstract space into a site of affective attachment and topophilic memory. Through Bachelard, she becomes a psychic dwelling, a poetic homecoming in which the intimate immensity of childhood, soil, colour and light is continually re-inhabited through painting. Yet she also embodies the risks of feminised landscape long critiqued by feminists, from Carolyn Merchant to Gillian Rose, the coding of land as woman, subject to a patriarchal gaze, possession and control. Against this, however, Paraskos's red woman rarely submits to passive availability. Her guarded gestures, ambiguous settings and defiant presence suggest instead what Rose has called paradoxical space, a representational field in which multiple and contradictory meanings coexist, destabilising the singular male narrative.

At the same time, Paraskos's direct engagement with Cypriot politics lends the red woman a contemporary urgency. She is not merely a mythical goddess or allegorical Venus of the past, but a figure through whom exile, erotic memory and the violent ruptures of Cypriot society today are still being negotiated on canvas. She fuses the personal and the collective, the erotic and the political, the mythical and the historical.

The red woman thus stands as a nexus of identity in Paraskos's oeuvre, the embodiment of Cyprus as place, spirit and memory. She is the bearer of exile and longing, and the site where patriarchal narratives of possession are both invoked and unsettled. She is at once muse and mother, victim and resistance fighter, an allegory and doppelgänger. In her shifting forms and contested meanings, Paraskos created a figure through which his own fractured sense of belonging could not only be represented but re-presented, and through which Cyprus itself could be imagined, not as a singular essence, but as a space of multiplicity, contradiction and eternal becoming.

Chapter 2:
London Can You Wait:
migration and identity

Stass Paraskos was the son of a peasant sheep farmer, born in the village of Anaphotia in eastern Cyprus. He had little schooling as a child, attending only primary school, and even then intermittently when he was not needed to help tend the family's flock of goats and sheep on the farm.

As an origin story this is very evocative, echoing that of the Italian artist Giotto allegedly being found by the celebrated early Renaissance master Cimabue, tending sheep in the Tuscan hills above Florence.[28] But the evocative quality can be misleading. It is perhaps more useful to latch onto another fact about the Paraskos origin story, one that links him not to the artists of the Italian Renaissance, but the vast majority of migrants who have travelled from one country to another over the centuries, in search of a new life, and continue to do so. That fact is that Paraskos came from

---

[28] This is a story that has its origins in Vasari's *Lives of the Artists* (1550)

a very poor background, and his decision to travel over two-thousand miles from Cyprus to Britain in 1953 was not born of a desire, or even vague hope, of becoming an artist. It was driven by poverty and the hope for a better life in a wealthier part of the British Empire than Cyprus. Indeed, a life in the centre of that empire, London. Nonetheless, this was still not a straightforward choice.

As Hélé Béji observes in *We, the Decolonized*, the encounter with the former imperial centre is charged with both longing and resentment. 'The presence of colonialism had cultivated in me a yearning for modernity, the thirst for civilisation,' she writes. 'Yet it was also the source of my self-hatred'.[29] The condition Béji describes, simultaneous attraction to and recoil from the colonial metropolis, captures something of the psychic tension that underlies Paraskos's migration from Cyprus to Britain. His decision to move was economic, but the imaginative geography that made Britain the destination of choice was itself a product of the colonialism.

---

[29] Hélé Beji, *L'Art contre la culture* (Paris: Éditions du Seuil, 1992) 33

When Paraskos arrived in London in 1953, with little money and few contacts, he had no choice but to work in cafés and restaurants, sweeping floors and washing dishes. And while he never worked in a fish and chip shop, he might well have done. He was a stranger in a strange land who had to work to survive, doing whatever he could turn his hand to.

Like many migrants to Britain in this period, the Paraskos story was fairly was typical. He was a beneficiary of the 1948 British Nationality Act, seeking a better life in Britain, which was then still described as the 'Mother Country'. Like the Windrush Generation, he was invited to come to Britain, but exactly what that invitation was to do was not clear. But let's inflect that statement slightly for greater accuracy and say instead that what that invitation was for him *to be* was not exactly clear.

In this chapter I want to look at the question of *being* for a migrant like Paraskos, as he moved from peasant farmer in Cyprus, to migrant worker in the food industry in England, and on to becoming an artist and university lecturer. The move was as surprising as it was rapid, but drawing partly on the ideas of Avtar

Brah and Stuart Hall I want to suggest that it required Paraskos to make conscious choices over his identity, indicating a high degree of agency in accepting and rejecting aspects of the outsider or migrant identity that could easily have dictated a very different path for him. Put another way, any notion of a pre-existing plot or narrative defining life as a migrant outsider had to be discarded by Paraskos in order to enable him to write a new narrative for himself as an artist. This is something we shall see Paraskos do. And yet there remains the question as to how much of his previous identity as a migrant outsider he was really able to discard in the face of arguably more powerful social forces determined to maintain his outsider identity.

Of all the immigrant groups arriving in Britain in the post-Second World War period, one of the least studied and least recognised is the community of Greek migrants from Cyprus. Cyprus, a British colony from 1878 until 1960, experienced significant emigration in the decades after the war. By the 1970s there were an estimated 85,000 Greek Cypriots living in Britain, most in London, a striking figure when set against the island's total Greek Cypriot population of around 600,000.[30] Although a proportion of this migration followed the events of 1974, when Turkey invaded and occupied almost 40 per cent of Cyprus, the majority had already arrived before that date. Many, like Paraskos, migrated under the terms of the 1948 British Nationality Act, seeking a better life.[31]

Despite the size of this community, its presence has often seemed invisible, particularly as later generations born in Britain assimilated into wider British society. The position of Greek Cypriots in Britain as a diaspora community is also complicated by appearance and religion. Generally, but not exclusively, light-skinned and Christian, their apparent affinities with the host culture may have smoothed assimilation in the long term. But this was not always the case. When the first large wave of Cypriot migrants, including Paraskos, arrived in the 1950s, they were often viewed with suspicion, not only because of

---

[30] Floya Anthias, *Ethnicity, Class, Gender and Migration: Greek-Cypriots in Britain* (London: Routledge, 1992) 5. This figure refers to those born in Cyprus.
[31] Richard T. Ashcroft and Mark Bevir, *Multiculturalism in the British Commonwealth* (University of California Press, 2019) 27

cultural differences, but due to the violent anti-colonial struggle then underway in Cyprus which claimed the lives of scores of British soldiers and civilians.[32] We might even posit that the now talismanic sign, said to hang outside numerous British guesthouses in the 1950s, reading 'No blacks, no Irish, no dogs' could in practice have been extended to read 'No Cypriots'.

Despite the scale of this migration, the Greek Cypriot experience in Britain remains curiously under-examined, and rarely acknowledged in post-colonial studies. A rare example is Kathy Burrell's 2005 oral history study of the Greek Cypriot population in Leicester. Being a much smaller diaspora community than London, the ability to create a fully-insular society in Leicester was not possible, but many of the clichés of the wider immigrant experience are still evident, including an emphasis on poverty and improvement based on hard work, and also experiences of racism. One of Burrell's interviewees made a comment that in Britain:

---

[32] Aaron Edwards, *Defending the Realm: The Politics of Britain's Small Wars since 1945* (Manchester: Manchester University Press, 2012) 126f

> Here we have been called all kinds of things, Paki, greasy, fuck off back to your own country, you name it, spat in the face. I've been called all kinds of things in this country. In the back of my mind, wherever I go, even on this street, I feel the racism on this street, I feel them looking at me, because I am on my own, I'm dark and I'm young. Everywhere I go I feel it. I don't go to pubs because I feel it as soon as I walk in, they look. You sense it because you have had it all your life.[33]

This aspect of the Greek Cypriot migrant experience is not something that appears explicitly in Paraskos's story, although it is reasonable to assume it was experienced by him in some way. I know from my personal experience, growing up in 1970s Britain, it was part of my story, and that of my siblings, in ways I recognise from the account of Burrell's interviewee. It is also not hard to believe it was at least a contributing

---

[33] Kathy Burrell, 'Urban Narratives: Italian and Greek-Cypriot Representations of Community in Post-War Leicester' in *Urban History* 32, no. 3 (December 2005) 481f

factor in the decision by the police to prosecute Paraskos in 1966 for exhibiting what they deemed were obscene and corrupting images. These comprised an oil painting and two drawings shown at an exhibition at Leeds College of Art. Particularly notable is that when the original charge was levelled, three defendants were accused, with the principal of the art school, Eric Taylor, and the tutor who ran the gallery, Patrick Hughes, also on the charge sheet alongside Paraskos. However, by the time of the trial only Paraskos, the immigrant and outsider, appeared in court to be found guilty. No explanation for this survives in the records and so we cannot be certain the decision on who to prosecute had a racial factor, but it is not inconceivable.

The question of explicit racism is similarly absent from another of the few large-scale studies of the Greek Cypriot experience in Britain, conducted by Pamela Constantinides in the mid-1970s. Focusing on the Greek Cypriot community in London, Constantinides found that its size enabled its members to maintain a strong insular culture that had only limited interaction with either the host society or other migrant communities. It was into this community that

Paraskos first settled in the early 1950s. Like many of his contemporaries, he entered one of the tropes of the Greek Cypriot migrant experience, the catering trade.[34] In his unpublished MPhil thesis of 1971, Cypriot migration and settlement in Britain, Robin Oakley notes that at that time the most common occupations of Greek Cypriot migrants 'are construction work, catering, and a number of traditional craft occupations such as tailoring, woodworking, hairdressing and shoemaking'.[35] This is echoed in the study of Greek Cypriots in Leicester by Burrell, as well as more tangential studies of the Greek Cypriot migrant experience, by writers such as Panikos Panayi.[36]

Paraskos migrated to Britain in 1953, when he was aged twenty. He recalled being given five pounds by his father and put on a boat to Brindisi in Italy. From there he travelled by a series of trains to London. When he arrived at Victoria Station, he later recounted, he thought he knew no one in the city. With only one

---

[34] Pamela Constantinides, 'Greek Cypriots' in J.L. Watson (ed.), *Between two cultures: migrants and minorities in Britain* (Oxford: Blackwell, 1977) 269f
[35] Robin Oakley, 'Cypriot Migration and Settlement in Britain,' unpublished MPhil thesis, University of Oxford (1971), 79
[36] Panikos Panayi, *Migrant City: A New History of London* (New Haven: Yale University Press, 2020) 79

pound left in his pocket and no clear idea where to go, he was not quite penniless, but still in a precarious situation. Then, what must have seemed like a miracle happened. As he walked down the platform he heard someone calling his name. Unknown to him, his father had written ahead to a member of the burgeoning Cypriot community in London, who was waiting there to meet him.

This tale of arrival is revealing, both in itself and in the way Paraskos chose to narrate it. In telling the story later, he often emphasised the elements of chance and serendipity, transforming the moment of salvation into something that reads almost like a medieval romance, with the hero facing grave danger only to be saved by providence. This makes the story resemble an act of emplotment, theorised by Hayden White as a narrative structure that shapes what appears to be a simple recounting of an historical event, but is in reality a partial narrative that follows a recognisable pattern or archetype. Paraskos's arrival story may read like the plot of a medieval romance, but it is also undercut by the insertion of another mode of emplotment, a comedic plot that reveals serendipity had nothing to do with this chance encounter on a railway platform. Rather his father had arranged the whole thing.

With both the romance plot and the comedic plot we see how emplotment not only establishes a kind of archetypal template into which real-life events are placed to give them a meaningful structure, but it requires elements to be excluded, or silenced, in order to maintain the narrative coherency of the tale. In this instance, to be seen as lost in the big city, Paraskos has to silence any reference to the fact he already had an older brother living in London, and any overt mention of the role of the existing Greek Cypriot community in receiving and supporting new arrivals from Cyprus, which might have come into play even without his father's letter. Migrant networks have long been crucial in helping newcomers find their way in a new setting, helping them to secure accommodation and obtain employment, and there is no reason to doubt the role of this community in helping Paraskos to settle in London. Even if low-paid work in London's catering sector was relatively easy to find in the 1950s, it seems likely that Paraskos's introductions to employers came through the

Cypriot community, already well established in the cafés and kitchens of Soho.

What this suggests to me is that the way Paraskos chose to frame his arrival story involves an element of self-mythologising, designed to present himself as already separate in some way from the Cypriot diaspora community in London, the archetypes of which did not include the concept of artist. By presenting his arrival as an isolated moment of peril and rescue, rather than as part of a collective pattern of migration and community support, Paraskos effectively distanced himself from the standard narrative of the Cypriot migrant experience and in so doing opened up the possibility for integration into an alternative community, or we might say an alternative narrative, namely that of the British art world.

This gets us to the crux of the matter. It is revealing to consider Paraskos's entry into the British art world in terms of emplotment, whereby the archetypal migrant plot he was forced into as a migrant entering Britain by necessity is rejected and replaced a new archetypal plot, namely that of the artist. I recognise we are stepping outside White's plot definitions with this nomenclature, but doing so enables us to hypothesise for Paraskos a move that is part social, part psychological and even part physical in that it required physical distancing from the migrant community of which he was initially a part. This would tally well with Partha Mitter's concept of 'Picasso manqué syndrome,' whereby artists from colonised regions are judged by how successfully they imitate the metropolitan forms of the centre.[37] Paraskos had to become, or imitate becoming, a Western artist. He could not be an immigrant *and* a Western artist. The problem lies in that word imitation. It also carries with it a sense of falsification, as though the adoption of the identity of Western artist can never truly be real of complete. For an artist like Paraskos, any manifestations of modernist form in his work risked being read not as full participation in Western modernism, but as imitation of it. Indeed, this dynamic would later underpin the reception of Paraskos as a 'naïve' artist rather than as an equal or peer within the British avant-garde.

---

[37] Partha Mitter, 'Decentering Modernism: Art History and Avant-Garde Art from the Periphery', in *The Art Bulletin,* vol. 90, no. 4 (December 2008) 537

As this suggests, even when a non-Western artist like Paraskos wants to embrace Western canonical discourses of art, they are not necessarily permitted to do so fully. But even gaining that partial level of integration into Western canonical discourses of art is no easy feat. At a personal level it results in loss at least as much as gain. In Béji's account of decolonisation, this kind of self-invention is inseparable from a kind of melancholic lucidity. She writes, 'Without such an affectively melancholic disposition... it would be impossible to uncreate and simultaneously create the conditions that make us agents of our own choices'.[38] Paraskos's deliberate remaking of his arrival story, its mixture of comedy and providence, can be read in this light: a performative gesture through which he dissolved one inherited plot (the peasant emigrant) to construct another (the modern artist). It involved as much loss as it offers any potential gain.

We can take this idea further by following Paraskos away from London, to the northern English

---

[38] Hélé Béji, *We, the Decolonized,* trans. Matthew B. Smith (Cambridge: Polity, 2025) 70

city of Leeds, where the actual point of disjuncture with his migrant narrative took place.

Paraskos moved to Leeds in 1956, initially to join his brother, who had married a woman whose father ran an Italian-style coffee shop in the city, called the Ritz. Before long, Paraskos and his brother were joined by the rest of their family from Cyprus and together they took over another restaurant in Leeds, the Montevideo, transforming it into the first Greek restaurant in the city. In this they benefited from the wave of bohemian philhellenism that swept Britain after the release of the film *Never on a Sunday* in 1960. This made the restaurant a popular gathering place for artists teaching at Leeds College of Art, among them the influential artist Harry Thubron.

The exact circumstances of the first encounter between Paraskos and Thubron is unclear, but out of their meeting came a suggestion from Thubron that Paraskos enrol at Leeds College of Art, despite his lack of qualifications. Indeed, the lack of qualifications was to prove an insurmountable barrier to Paraskos formally enrolling at the school, with Thubron being forced instead to arrange for him to attend classes unofficially. As a result, although Paraskos attended Leeds College of Art he never gained an academic qualification from there, a fact that never stood in the way of him being employed to teach at numerous universities in Britain and elsewhere over the next five decades.[39] For our purposes, what matters here is that this meeting led to Paraskos embracing the life of an art student and, soon after, the life of an artist. This moment is a crucial inflection point in the Paraskos story. The narrative trajectory we might have expected him to follow, of a migrant working in the catering industry, a path taken by the vast majority of Greek Cypriot migrants to Britain, was dramatically altered. But what I want to suggest is that this inflection required him to make a break with the migrant community, effectively to rewrite his own narrative plot, to enable him to enter into a very different community, that of the British art world.

---

[39] Technically, even today, a university in Britain does not require tutors to have a degree or other qualification to teach, although it is rare for this to happen today. Paraskos did not gain his first university qualification until 2008, when he was awarded an honorary doctorate from the University of Bolton for services to art education.

From this point on, Paraskos's engagement with the radical art world emerging in Britain, primarily in the northern English art schools, in the 1950s and 60s, had all the hallmarks of a break with his past. The values and mores of the community of artists he joined diverged significantly from the socially-conservative ones held by the Greek Cypriot community at the time, including those in the migrant diaspora. Unlike his brothers, two of whom helped establish a new Greek Orthodox church in Leeds, Paraskos was also distanced from much of the migrant Greek Cypriot community through his atheism and frequently overt hostility to the Greek church, one of the linchpins of the community in Britain. In this we have something that resembles what we see in a writer like V.S. Naipaul, who claimed he needed to break with his Trinidadian past in order to become a Western writer. In his 1983 essay 'Our Universal Civilization' Naipaul stated, 'To be an artist, I knew I had to go to the centre, to London, to the metropolis.'[40] Similarly, in an interview in 2000 with *The Guardian* newspaper, Naipaul again said, 'You have

---

[40] V. S. Naipaul, 'Our Universal Civilization' in *The New York Review of Books*, 31 January 1991

to make yourself anew. You have to shed all the chains of that background. You cannot be sentimental. You have to be brutal.'[41]

Yet, with Paraskos, this would be an oversimplification. Paraskos remained a Greek Cypriot, never renouncing his identity completely, and so we might want a more subtle conceptualisation of how he negotiated, or rewrote, his relationship with the migrant Greek Cypriot community in Britain. In this we should perhaps consider Paraskos in the context of Avtar Brah's conceptualisation of diaspora spaces. Through Brah we might put aside the idea of the Greek Cypriot community in Britain being a single entity, despite its remarkable degree of community cohesion. Brah suggests that rather than seeing migrant communities as singular, homogenous and unchanging wholes we need to recognise that they too are subject to processes of change and internal divergence. What might be viewed from outside as a single migrant community, evident in the way in which government and media will often talk about community leaders, should really be considered a

---

[41] V. S. Naipaul, quoted in 'The Enigma of Arrival,' interview with Rachel Donadio, *The Guardian*, 18 August 2000

'diaspora space' in which migrant communities navigate, negotiate and renegotiate over time both their internal relationships and their relationships with the outside world. So, while a migrant community might collectively be labelled the Greek-Cypriot community, it will have internal differences and divisions, and its members have different relationships with external forces.

This dynamism within the diaspora space results in what Brah calls *creolisation*. She suggests that internal change and external encounters lead to a series of borders within the diaspora space, each every bit as important as any border differentiating the migrant community from other migrant communities and the host country. Brah writes:

> Diaspora space is the intersectionality of diaspora, border, and dis/location as a point of confluence of economic, political, cultural, and psychic processes. It is where multiple subject positions are juxtaposed, contested, proclaimed or disavowed; where the permitted and the prohibited perpetually interrogate; and where

the accepted and the transgressive
imperceptibly mingle even while these syncretic
forms may be disclaimed in the name of purity
and tradition. Here, tradition is itself
continually invented even as it may be hailed as
originating from the mists of time. What is at
stake is the infinite experientiality, the myriad
processes of cultural fissure and fusion that
underwrite contemporary forms of
transcultural identities. These emergent
identities may only be surreptitiously avowed.
Indeed, they may even be disclaimed or
suppressed in the face of constructed
imperatives of 'purity'. But they are inscribed
in the late twentieth-century forms of
syncretism at the core of culture and
subjectivity.[42]

Applying this theory to Paraskos suggests that we look at the encounter with Thubron at the Montevideo restaurant, and his subsequent entry into

---

[42] Avtar Brah, *Cartographies of Diaspora: Contesting Identities* (London: Routledge, 1996) 208

the connected worlds of art student, artist and art lecturer as evidence of creolisation, which is to say, as the renegotiation by Paraskos of his relationship with the migrant community. Given the level of divergence between the socially-conservative Cypriot migrant community and the socially-liberal art world of Britain in the 1950s and 60s, this meant a high degree of potential discord between the two, which may have the effect of looking like Paraskos made a definitive break with his identity as a migrant. Indeed, perhaps he wanted to, but the individual will always face social pressures from more powerful forces that makes that an extremely difficult thing to achieve.

Part of the resistance to making a definitive break will come from within the migrant community itself. According to Brah aspects of both internally and externally-induced creolisation have the potential to be disclaimed or suppressed by the migrant community's dominant and most powerful voices, often in the name of purity and tradition.[43] With Paraskos it is not hard to see the difficulty in reconciling an identity rooted in

---

[43] Avtar Brah, *Cartographies of Diaspora: Contesting Identities* (London: Routledge, 1996) 208

traditional Cypriot values of the time with that of the increasingly radicalised modernist art world evident in Britain in the 1950s and 60s. The Greek Cypriot diaspora space was never a likely environment for exercising the ideas of absolute freedom of action or thought increasingly evident in that art world, and it is tempting to draw a parallel between aspects of Paraskos's experience, and the fictionalised representation of the art student, Tariq, in in Ayub Khan-Din's play (and later film) *East is East,* set in Salford in 1971. As we have heard, in 1966 Paraskos was arrested and prosecuted for exhibiting paintings deemed obscene. In *East is East* the art student Tariq, the son of the Pakistani migrant, George Khan, shocks his brother's conservative prospective mother-in-law with the sculpture of a vagina he has made at art school. Of course, there is a key difference with Paraskos as the potential rupture with the dominant values of the diaspora space in *East is East* is through a so-called second-generation migrant, Tariq. But in many respects we can see Paraskos as almost acting like a second-generation migrant in the tensions between his diaspora community and the lure of an aspect of the host community, although as Brah notes these tensions need to be conceptualised in terms of 'configurations of power' both internally within the diaspora space, as well as in relation to the power structures of the dominant culture.[44]

It is difficult to gauge the degree to which Paraskos was conscious of any moves to distance himself from the Greek Cypriot diaspora community, but even if not deliberate, he can still be seen to deviate from a standard path of the migrant experience, and in that as rejecting the standard identity narrative of plot of a migrant. The identity he sought to adopt instead was that of an artist in the British art world. In saying this, it is worth noting that neither the migrant identity nor that of the artist is synonymous with normative British or English identity. Consequently, both identities carried something of a marginal, or outsider, status, albeit for different reasons. Clearly this has the potential to create intersections of marginality, with potentially catastrophic consequences. Indeed, we could argue this

---

[44] Avtar Brah, *Cartographies of Diaspora: Contesting Identities* (London: Routledge, 1996) 208

is exactly what we do see with the Paraskos trial for obscenity in 1966.

On paper, transition between one culture and another might appear easy, but the point about Ayub Khan-Din's *East is East*, and the experience of Paraskos, is that it is not. Indeed, Paraskos acknowledged this difficulty. Speaking to Christina Lambrou in 2013 he said, 'I had a hard time getting in (to the British art world) because I didn't speak English well.' Nonetheless, he also noted that artists tend to be friendly and so he made friends in the art world easily.[45] In this, I think we get a sense of Paraskos almost seeking access to a community in which he would not be judged over his perceived native Britishness or alien Cypriotness, let alone the quality of his spoken English, but simply for his artistic ability. We can argue Paraskos was attempting to shape his own migrant narrative away from what Stuart Hall has identified as hegemonic structures, or scripts, towards a far more fluvial cultural identity. That identity did not necessarily

---

[45] Χριστίνα Λάμπρου "Συνέντευξη στη Στας Παράσκος' in *Politis*, 28 October 2013. Online version https://www.parathyro.politis.com.cy/features/interviews/145584/parathyro.politis.com.cy

eschew his Cypriotness, in the manner described by
Naipaul, but it also did not accept a singular or passive
understanding of that identity. Indeed, in the same
interview in which Paraskos spoke of the difficulty he
had in getting into the British art world, he gave a clear
indication as to why he still sought entry to that world.
'Imagine coming from a village in Cyprus,' he said,
'with its restrictions, habits, customs, and traditions, and
suddenly finding a circle of complete freedom.'[46] In
short, he was seeking a way out of the narrative plot of
Cypriotness, as defined both by most Cypriots
themselves and the host country's view of Cyprus.

    A sense of how restrictive the Cypriot diaspora
community in London might have seemed in the 1950s
and 60s is gained from Pamela Constantinides's
important study into Greek Cypriot diaspora culture in
London, published in 1977. Drawn from interviews
conducted in both Cyprus and London just before and
after the war between Cyprus and Turkey in 1974, it
charted attitudes towards integration into the host
country by London Greek Cypriots. Constantinides
noted that prior to the large influx of Greek Cypriots

---

[46] *Ibid.*

into Britain in the late 1950s, there was a belief and fear amongst Cypriots who remained in Cyprus that those who left would lose their identity, a process called 'ethnic disappearance'. Young men in particular were viewed as in danger of being lost to the community through marriage to English women. According to Constantinides this danger was ameliorated from the later 1950s onwards by the sheer number of Greek Cypriots in London, which enabled the community to maintain a high level of internal cultural coherency by social limitations being placed on interactions with the host culture. Mostly this was evident in who émigré Cypriots married, but it also extended to where they lived, worshipped and socialised, and even where they shopped and worked.[47] In effect, Constantinides's report suggests that the 'village in Cyprus, with its restrictions, habits, customs and traditions' that Paraskos was keen to escape was imported wholesale into London in the late 1950s by Cypriot émigrés.

It is not hard to see how the distance between the London Greek Cypriot diaspora and Paraskos

---

[47] Pamela Constantinides, 'Greek Cypriots' in J.L. Watson (ed.), *Between two cultures: migrants and minorities in Britain* (Oxford: Blackwell, 1977) 298

would grow to the point where, when he returned to London from Leeds in 1967, he did not re-enter the diaspora space but went instead into the heart of the British contemporary world, the Institute of Contemporary Arts (ICA). As already mentioned, the previous year Paraskos had provoked a scandal by being arrested for exhibiting supposedly obscene paintings at an exhibition in Leeds. The worldwide notoriety resulting from the trial led to Paraskos being invited to exhibit alongside Pat Douthwaite, Ian Dury, Herbert Kitchen, and Graham Ovenden at the ICA, in a group show entitled *Fantasy and Figuration*. As Norbert Lynton later wrote, 'Today we are all more relaxed about these things, and the accused might well be heroicised by the media. Even then, the press, reporting the trial, seemed surprised at the fuss.'[48] But that is not to say the 'fuss' would have played well in the socially-conservative Greek-Cypriot diaspora community, or even the community back in Cyprus. Although we have no evidence as to how the wider Cypriot community viewed the Paraskos trial, we do know that when Paraskos returned to Cyprus for a visit in 1968, the

---

[48] Norbert Lynton, *Stass Paraskos* (London: Orage Press, 2003) 18

morality of himself, his family and friends was questioned in the local press.[49]

Yet for an émigré artist like Paraskos, assimilation into the British art world was also never a straightforward matter. Inclusion depended not only on self-determination but also on the terms set by the art world's gatekeepers. As Stuart Hall has observed, migrant artists are often confined within hegemonic scripts of ethnicity and integration, narratives that dictate how their work should be read and what identities they are permitted to inhabit.[50] This is something evident in the experience of the Karachi-born artist Rasheed Araeen, an exact contemporary of Paraskos, who encountered very directly the limits of acceptance. Araeen's sculptural works, though conceived by him to be in dialogue with international modernism, have been frequently framed by Western critics through the lens of Islamic geometric pattern or South Asian heritage, sometimes termed the 'folkloric trap'. These are categories that mark out a sense of

---

[49] See Appendix A
[50] Stuart Hall, 'Cultural Identity and Diaspora,' in Jonathan Rutherford (ed.) *Identity: Community, Culture, Difference* (London: Lawrence & Wishart, 1990) 222–237

difference rather than artistic parity. As Araeen has noted in numerous writings, the label 'international modernist' appears reserved by art historians, critics and curators for white Western artists alone.[51]

Consequently, although Paraskos's work absorbed influences from friends such as the artists Alan Davie and Terry Frost, and he experimented with the formal division of pictorial space in ways that had affinities with formalist abstraction, the reading of his work has almost universally focused on figurative and narrative content that is more readily explained in terms of his Cypriot background. This was the point which made contemporary critics, such as Merete Bates, repeatedly frame Paraskos as a 'naïve' or 'peasant' artist, a label that tethered his practice to an ethnicised and folkloric reading rather than recognising it as a conscious, contemporary intervention that engaged with and challenged Western art as much as it embraced it.[52] Such framing exemplifies what Hall has identified as the hegemonic scripts of ethnicity, a

---

[51] Rasheed Araeen, 'A New Beginning: Beyond Postcolonial Cultural Theory and Identity Politics,' in *Third Text* 14, no. 50 (Spring 2000) 5
[52] Merete Bates 'Stass Paraskos' in *The Guardian*, 22 May 1970, 8

cultural shorthand that fixes migrant artists into predetermined roles, regardless of the meaning and complexity of their practice.

It would also be a mistake to assume this was an attitude that belongs only in the past. In Derek Horton's review of a 2016 retrospective of Paraskos's work at The Tetley art space in Leeds, Horton explicitly discounted any suggestion Paraskos might have been a radical figure in the modernist mould. While emphasising that his paintings possessed a 'naïve charm,' Horton claimed they 'do little to test any real boundaries.'[53] Like Bates, Horton's framing diminished Paraskos's authority and artistic ambition, echoing a classic Orientalising manoeuvre in which a subject's complexity is contracted into notions of charming folkloric excess. This obscures any latent conceptual or political forces and creates a critical impasse in which we are faced with the illogical claim that works which provoked police action, a high-profile trial and the condemnation of the British judiciary are deemed to be

---

[53] Derek Horton, 'Jonathan Trayte: Polyculture / Stass Paraskos: Lovers and Romances,' in *Corridor8* (review, 22 August 2016), online at https://corridor8.co.uk/article/review-jonathan-trayte-polyculture-stass-paraskos-lovers-and-romances-the-tetley-leeds/

un-radical. The only possible solution to this situation is to recognise that the discrepancy lies not in Paraskos's work, but in the critical narrative framework Horton sought to apply. By judging the paintings in a way detached from their social context, he replicated the act of de-contextualisation that the emplotment of naïveté requires. Therefore, the review becomes evidence of the framework's power to overwrite historical fact with a more palatable, and less challenging, artistic identity. But more than this, Horton's analysis exemplifies the way the white Western gaze flattens the art of non-Western artists into quaint artefacts, a process that, as Araeen has argued, systematically silences the disruptive dissonances introduced by artists working within hybrid modernist language.[54] With Paraskos, this specifically silences the real dissonances Paraskos introduced into the British art world through his hybrid visual language and transgressive narratives.

It is clear that Araeen actively resisted such framing of his practice, most notably through the founding of *Third Text*, but it is also possible to argue

---

[54] Rasheed Araeen, *Art and Institutional Racism* (London: Austin Macauley, 2024) especially 25f and 51f

that Paraskos also sought to resist attempts to define him through the Western gaze. That gaze repeatedly sets up binaries between the viewer and viewed (the gazer and the object of the gaze), defining itself and the object as the contrasting opposites of each other. We shall see this later in relation to Paraskos's marginalisation by the Netherlands-based Manifesta organisation when it attempted to stage an event in Cyprus in 2006, but this resistance also appeared elsewhere. When Paraskos represented Cyprus at the São Paulo Biennale in 1996, he wrote that Cyprus belonged to a very different artistic zone from that of Western art, noting that 'all creativity does not begin and end with North America and Europe.'[55] For him, Cyprus occupied a cultural space in which the European (Greek) and African (Egyptian) traditions historically met, an almost matrixial zone distinct from the fixed and patriarchal positions of the West.

This resonates with other radical reappraisals of the modernist project that have emerged from non-

---

[55] Stass Paraskos 'Personal Statement' in Eleni Nikita, *Stass Paraskos at the 23rd International Biennial of São Paulo 1996* (Nicosia: Ministry of Culture, 1996) 7

Western sources. In particular it parallels the call by Partha Mitter to 'shift the centre of gravity of modernism,' in order to recover the counter-discourses emerging from what Mitter calls the peripheries. It is these pluralistic, heterogeneous modernisms that challenge the singular and linear Euro-American narrative.[56] Paraskos's articulation of Cyprus as a matrixial zone between Europe and Africa can be read as such a counter-modernist gesture, a local modernity asserting parity with, rather than binary dependence on, a self-defined metropolitan centre in the West.

This also corresponds closely to what Stuart Hall has called the new ethnicities that arise through migration and diasporic settlement in new cultural contexts. Artists such as Araeen and Paraskos rejected the Orientalist and folkloric identities imposed upon them, instead enacting a heterogeneous culture formed through continual interaction with others. As Hall argued, what defines the new ethnicities is a belief and practice in which cultural identity is not a fixed essence but an unstable point of identification made 'within the

---

[56] Partha Mitter, 'Decentering Modernism: Art History and Avant-Garde Art from the Periphery' in *The Art Bulletin*, Vol. 90, No. 4, December 2008, 540

discourses of history and culture.'[57] In this light, both Araeen and Paraskos can be seen to have refused the hegemonising forms of ethnic identity generated by the Western gaze. Their identities were, of necessity, heterogeneous, diverse and hybrid, in marked contrast to the Western gaze.

Paraskos's statement for the 23rd San Paulo Biennale indicates this was an intentional political act. His coarse language in the statement might offend some academic sensibilities, but Paraskos was not an academic and his language can also be seen as a rejection of Western canonical forms. From a post-colonial perspective, the refusal of Paraskos to conform to the hegemonic narrative of Western modernism can be read as an act of resistance, one that asserted the validity of an alternative modernism grounded in the new ethnicity of diverse cultural memories and environments arising from a location that had itself been colonised by the very metropole whose art world he now inhabited. Crucially it asserts that if he was

---

[57] *Stuart Hall, 'Cultural Identity and Diaspora' in Jonathan Rutherford (ed.) Identity: Community, Culture, Difference* (London: Lawrence & Wishart, 1990) 225

been seen within a narrative plot or framework, Paraskos was not willing to let others define the nature of that plot, least of all according to Western clichés of his identity. Instead, he asserted his own agency.

As a result we have to recognise that seeing Paraskos as a folkloric or naïve artist is wrong. But also wrong is the notion that he merely hybridised Western modernism with elements of Cypriot culture to produce some kind of artistic chimaera. Both readings reduce his work to the terms of an existing script, a narrative plot he rejected. What emerges instead is evidence of an artistic practice that refused to settle into any singular category, modernist or traditional, Western or Cypriot, and which derived its force precisely from that refusal. In a space between identities, Paraskos created a body of work with narratives, imagery and formal strategies that articulated a self-determined position, one that neither rejected nor passively inherited his cultural origins, but instead continually reconfigured them in dialogue with, and often in opposition to, the dominant currents of the Western art world.

Chapter 3:
I Fought the Law:
censorship and the politics of marginality

In April 1966 Paraskos found himself under arrest by the City of Leeds Police for an exhibition of his paintings and drawings held at the Leeds Institute Gallery, the in-house art gallery of Leeds College of Art. He was not alone on the charge sheet, with both the principal of the art school, Eric Taylor, and the tutor responsible for overseeing the gallery, Patrick Hughes, also in the frame.[58] It might be significant that when the case came to court the following December, only Paraskos was placed in the dock.

To describe the charges as ridiculous is not simply a case of changing values in the intervening decades. Even in 1966, at the height of the period known as the 'swinging sixties', when Britain was being swept by new liberal attitudes, the arrest of Paraskos seemed to many to be absurd. Not only were his paintings produced in a non-naturalistic style that made

---

[58] Patrick Hughes is also known as Peter Hughes.

them unlikely material for any passing onanist, the tradition of nudity in art was well-established, not least in the extensive public art collections of the City of Leeds itself. Indeed, in the records of the affair, held at the National Archives in Kew, there is a letter to the Chief Constable of Leeds City Police, from the Director of Public Prosecutions, Maurice Crump, expressing 'regret' at news the local police had decided to pursue the case. Separately Crump noted, 'I feel that it would be absurd to have recourse to the criminal law in a matter of this kind.'[59]

The works of art themselves were part of a narrative sequence, not untypical of Paraskos's tendency throughout his life to present thematic shows through his work. In the case a couple meet, fall in love, make love and part. Included were images of the couple, but also of animals copulating, presumably intended to evoke both the physical and spiritual aspects of love, expressed in Greek as *eros* (desire, passionate love) and *agape* (selfless, transcendent love). Drawing in part on expressionist visual traditions, none of the images can be described as naturalistic. The

---

[59] National Archives, Kew, London, DPP2/4193

painting titled in the trial *Lost Love*, but now more often referred to by the exhibition title, *Lovers and Romances*, depicts a young couple on the left, naked and making love, while on the right the male figure reappears, older, more portly, and alone. At the bottom left of the image the couple are shown again, possibly earlier in their courtship, their bodies absent so that only their heads are visible, the woman blushing profusely. If this vignette is of their first meeting and suggests the spiritual dimension of *agape*, we can perhaps read their lovemaking as the physical impulse of *eros*, with the sequence concluding with the older man reflecting on his lost love. This may seem an excessively intellectual interpretation of the painting,[60] but the point I want to emphasise is that it stages three phases of love, an ideal *agape*, a physical *eros*, and finally a nostalgic yearning, all within a resolutely abstract setting that is relevant to the Paraskos trial. Together with the abstract forms of the background, it is abundantly clear that we are not meant to read this image as a representation of reality. Indeed, it would be difficult to do so.

---

[60] See Anders Nygren, *Agape and Eros* (Chicago: University of Chicago Press, 1982)

This point was raised during the trial by one of the witnesses for the defence, Norbert Lynton, then art critic of *The Guardian* newspaper. Recalling the event later, Lynton wrote:

> The nine expert witnesses (for the defence) agreed on the high quality of Paraskos's work. We stressed its poetic, unrealistic character. Some of us emphasised the special value of showing what the prosecution had called 'love-play' in a context of tenderness when sexual relationships are so frequently shown or described in terms of violence and fortuity.

To this he added, 'We insisted on the stylised, generalised quality of these works, and suggested that the timelessness of art lifted such subjects onto a different plane.'[61]

Unfortunately for Paraskos this line of defence was not accepted by the court. Although Paraskos may have intended the images to operate within an idealised

---

[61] Norbert Lynton, 'Art and the Expert Witness', in *The Guardian*, 5 January 1967, 7

alternative reality, the court insisted that the images in the exhibition could only be judged in terms of somatic depiction. This made any defence extremely difficult as the laws under which Paraskos was charged, the Vagrancy Acts 1823 and 1837, did not permit a defence based on artistic values.

The exhibition opened on 25 April 1966 and was scheduled to run until 12 May. On 28 April the gallery was raided by police constables George Edward Jew and Jack Underwood. In his statement of 11 May, P.C. Jew noted that a complaint had been made, although he did not identify the source. Out of an exhibition containing 'approximately sixty-five works,' Jew identified two that he considered obscene, the painting *Lost Love* and a black-and-white drawing. His statement read:

> I examined the paintings on display and Exhibit No. 45 (Lost Love) portrayed a naked man on the right of the painting, and on the left was a naked man and woman who were

kissing each other, the woman was shown to be holding what appeared to be the man's penis.[62]

Looking at the National Archives file it appears that the Director of Public Prosecutions, Maurice Crump, moved quickly to try to prevent the case from going to trial. Writing to, John Hetherington, the Chief Constable of Leeds City Police, on 18 May, Crump made clear that prosecuting Paraskos under the 1959 Obscene Publications Act was unlikely to succeed, since Section 4 of the Act did allow for a defence on the grounds of artistic merit, the so-called *public good* defence. But Crump also advised against prosecution under the Vagrancy Acts, explaining that:

> The provisions of Section 4 of the Vagrancy Act are intended for a different purpose, not to protect the community from being corrupted but to protect them from having thrust upon their sight things which are offensive to them.[63]

---

[62] National Archives, Kew, London, DPP2/4193
[63] *Ibid.*

Here the issue as to whether the exhibition was in a public space proved decisive. If a member of the public accidentally encountered the exhibition and found themselves confronted with nudity without warning, the Vagrancy Act could arguably apply. However, if the gallery was considered a private space, part of an art school not normally open to the general public, then the matter was less straightforward. Either way, the tone of Crump's correspondence with Hetherington, and his later expression of disappointment that the prosecution was to proceed despite his warnings, indicate that he wished the matter to be dropped. In a letter of 2 August he added pointedly: 'I would also observe that the whole matter is now somewhat stale and therefore liable to criticism in that respect.'[64]

Crump's private view was even clearer. Writing to child psychologist Dr Wilfred Warren of London's Maudsley Hospital on 24 May, he remarked: 'I feel that it would be absurd to have recourse to the criminal law in a matter of this kind.' Nonetheless, he asked Warren for a professional opinion as to whether Paraskos's work

---

[64] National Archives, Kew, London, DPP2/4193

might corrupt or deprave its viewers. Warren's reply was sardonic but unequivocal:

> I cannot consider that any of these pictures are likely to deprave or corrupt young persons or even children. They might learn something of 'the facts of life' from them, but they would not in my opinion thereby be harmed.[65]

With such strong opposition from the highest legal circles in London, the question remains why Paraskos was prosecuted at all. Within the Leeds context, the attitude of the local police, particularly the Chief Constable, appears crucial. In the mid-1960s the police acted as the primary prosecuting body in criminal cases. However, attention can also be directed towards the local Watch Committee. These were local committees comprising councillors and lay magistrates which held oversight of the police in each area. Its outlook and influence may have shaped the decision to proceed. But there was also the broader picture arising

---

[65] National Archives, Kew, London, DPP2/4193

from resistance to what was seen as the increasing liberalisation of British society.

In 1960 Penguin Books had helped usher in the liberal society by publishing a paperback edition of D. H. Lawrence's novel *Lady Chatterley's Lover*, which depicted an affair between a married aristocratic woman and her gardener. First printed privately in Florence in 1928, its importation into Britain and sale had been banned until the passing of the Obscene Publications Act in 1959. As we have heard, this introduced the possibility of a defence on the grounds of artistic merit. The passing of the Act led to Penguin issuing a British edition of Lady Chatterly, which in turn led to an immediate prosecuted for obscenity. The ensuing court case was won by Penguin in what was viewed as a serious blow to Britain's self-appointed conservative guardians of public morality.

Despite this, those guardians of public morality continued to fight against what they saw as an increasingly permissive society. In 1963 an unsuccessful attempt was made to ban Henry Miller's *Tropic of Cancer* and a partially successful one to maintain a longstanding ban on John Cleland's novel *Fanny Hill*.

The ban on publication of this book had been in place for two centuries and was in fact not lifted until 1970.

The attack on Miller is of particular interest in relation to Paraskos as it was seen by some as revenge for the *Lady Chatterley* verdict. Chief Superintendent Kennedy of Scotland Yard made this plain when he wrote:

> The publication of this book affords an opportunity to mount a counter-attack to avenge the repulse we have suffered in the Lady Chatterley case. In my opinion, and I do not speak without experience, in the light of modern trends, and certainly from our own aspect, no effort or expense should be spared to mount such a counter-attack, and thus vindicate the attitude of the vast majority of our populace.[66]

As this suggests, a significant body within the establishment, including the police, was determined to prosecute writers and their publishers in an effort to

---

[66] Alan Travis, *Bound and Gagged* (London: Profile Books, 2001) 176

halt the march of the permissive society. By 1966 this determination had extended to the visual arts, with attempted prosecutions that year, not only of Paraskos, but also Jim Dine[67] and, in a curious echo of the attack on the venerable *Fanny Hill*,[68] the Victoria and Albert Museum for exhibiting work by the long-dead Victorian artist Aubrey Beardsley.[69]

With this context, in asking why Paraskos was prosecuted in 1966 we are brought face to face with a conservative establishment intent on making examples of those who dared to challenge its moral code. To do that required neutralising any suggestion that art had a special licence when it came to depicting the human body and human interactions, and successfully labelling any putative transgressors as no different to pornographers. Effectively, Paraskos and the other artists and writers prosecuted in the mid-1960s had to be presented as pornographers rather than artists, so that the emplotment of their motivations was moved

---

[67] John A. Walker *Art and Outrage* (London: Pluto Press, 1999) 47
[68] Alan Travis, *Bound and Gagged* (London: Profile Books, 2001) 184
[69] The attempted prosecution of the Victoria and Albert Museum for this exhibition was in fact halted by the Director of Public Prosecutions. See Alan Travis, *Bound and Gagged* (London: Profile Books, 2001) 199f

from being governed by a creative impulse to a desire to profit from corruption and depravity.

It is clear that even at the time Paraskos understood this was the underlying political motivation of those attacking him. Reading the official police file now lodged at the National Archives in Kew, the obscenity trial can appear phlegmatic and unemotional, as if a simple process was being carried through to its logical conclusion. Emotion surfaces only briefly, in the suggestion that two schoolgirls present during P.C. Jew's raid were seen giggling at one of the offending pictures, although notably P.C. Jew did not make this claim in his original report. There is emotion too in the evident frustration of Crump as he tried, unsuccessfully, to prevent the prosecution.[70] Writing some forty years later, Norbert Lynton reflected:

> We did our best to sound reasonable…It was all a waste of time. 'Mr Paraskos' was found guilty. It was said the pictures would be destroyed, but in fact they were returned t o him and a fine

---

[70] National Archives, Kew, London, DPP2/4193

> was imposed. Not too grave a matter? It lives
> on in Stass's mind.[71]

But if emotion is absent from the official record, it is patently evident in Paraskos's response. In one of the earliest newspaper reports of the trial, in May 1966, Paraskos is quoted as saying he was 'shocked' at his arrest.[72] A year later, in April 1967, he wrote a vitriolic attack in *The Leicester Mercury* on the British state, arguing that the laws governing censorship and pornography had not only become obsolete, but positively dangerous, rewarding artists who transgressed them with notoriety, rather than for the merit of their art. This risked, he warned, producing 'Cop Art,' with artists making work simply to provoke any passing policeman into action. Turning his ire on the Director of Public Prosecutions, Paraskos accused him of permitting prosecutions to proceed under the Vagrancy Acts as a way of evading the artistic defence afforded by the revised Obscene Publications Act, thereby giving

---

[71] Norbert Lynton, *Stass Paraskos* (London: Orage Press, 2003) 18
[72] *The Daily Mirror*, 30 April 1966, 2

'ammunition to philistinism and hypocrisy masquerading as the man in the street.'[73]

It is clear Paraskos was unaware of Crump's attempts to prevent his case from going to trial. In reality, a war of attrition was under way within the British establishment over the permissive society. As Allan Travis has charted in *Bound and Gagged*, every move to liberalise the law and its enforcement, particularly under Harold Wilson's Labour government in the second half of the 1960s, was met with a counter-move by those determined to resist.[74] This ranged from use of archaic laws, such as the Vagrancy Acts, to prosecute artists, as in Paraskos's case, to highly visible public morality campaigns conducted by figures such as Mary Whitehouse against playwright Dennis Potter and the BBC, even when no lawbreaking was involved.[75]

This dovetails with media coverage of the trial, which was both extensive and international. Taking place at a time when Britain had a much more vibrant

---

[73] *Leicester Mercury*, 18 April 1968, 12
[74] Alan Travis, *Bound and Gagged* (London: Profile Books, 2001) 166f
[75] See 'Arts Guardian' in *The Guardian*, 16 February 1973, 10

regional press than now, the story of the trial appeared not only in local and national newspapers but also in overseas media and art magazines.

In the national press early notice of the exhibition came in a review in *The Guardian* by M.G. McNay. Although published after Paraskos's arrest, McNay made no reference to the trial or to the fact that the exhibition had been closed by the police, suggesting the piece had been filed with the editor some days earlier. Praising Paraskos, McNay observed: 'Just as one is beginning to wonder whether one is becoming blasé… along comes a painter like Stass Paraskos.' Instead of mentioning the works that had offended P.C. Jew, McNay singled out a large painting of the artist Robin Page and his wife Carol, describing it as, 'packed with detail and patterning, yet (giving) an impression of total simplicity: a great feat of visual organisation.'[76]

Early coverage of the arrest itself in the national press can be seen in an article published in *The Daily Mirror*. This report led with comments from Paraskos himself, quoting him as saying, 'I am absolutely shocked. The exhibition has the support of

---

[76] *The Guardian*, 7 May 1966, 6

the local education committee and people in authority must have seen the pictures.' This in itself is interesting as it indicates Paraskos's state of mind in the first few days after the arrest, suggesting a sense of bafflement. Prefiguring the argument he would use the following year in his angry article in *The Leicester Mercury*, Paraskos is also quoted as saying, 'the pictures that have been withdrawn do not depict perverted love — they are quite wholesome.'[77]

In Britain's regional press a typical example of the tone of reporting can be seen in Liverpool's *Echo* in its initial account of the arrest. The report from 29 April 1966 is largely factual in terms of the charges, but quotes the Principal of Leeds College of Art, Eric Taylor, as saying:

> I would not regard them as being in any way indecent or obscene. It is a matter of appreciation of art. Only an uncultured and an uneducated mind could imagine this sort of thing.[78]

---

[77] *The Daily Mirror*, 30 April 1966, 2
[78] *Liverpool Echo*, 29 April 1966, 1

In *The Leicester Mercury* the following day Eric Taylor's quotation was again used, alongside Paraskos's more inflammatory claim that his arrest was 'absolutely stupid.'[79] The re-use of quotations suggests the arrest and trial was covered by a small number of reporters whose copy was then syndicated to the local and national press, as well as to a large number of overseas newspapers. This led to reports of the trial appearing repeatedly in such unlikely newspapers as *The Flint Journal* of Michigan and the *St Joseph News-Press* in Missouri, to name just two of numerous examples. Quite what the residents of Cleveland, Ohio made of the story of a Greek-Cypriot artist being arrested for showing nude paintings in an English city called Leeds is anyone's guess, but they could have read about it on page 44 of their local newspaper, *The Plain Dealer,* on the morning of Sunday 1 May 1966.

Between the arrest in April and the actual trial in December 1966 media coverage almost disappeared. Indeed, in one of the rare articles to appear in this interim, in *The Guardian* on 21 September 1966, this

---

[79] *Leicester Mercury,* 30 April 1966, 11

disappearance from the media landscape was noted. Headlined 'Stass's last stand,' the piece compared the Paraskos case to the police raid on another exhibition of paintings, by the American artist Jim Dine, at the Robert Fraser Gallery in London, the same year. As *The Guardian* observed, the Paraskos case was receiving far less publicity, despite the artist being 'determined to put up a fight.' *The Guardian* went on to list some of the prominent expert witnesses scheduled to appear for the defence, including 'Sir Herbert Read, Quentin Bell and Norbert Lynton.' It ended with almost relish, remarking that the Paraskos trial had 'the makings of a "Chatterley" case for the art world.'[80]

Interest in the trial also re-emerged briefly in October, when Paraskos was summoned to appear at Leeds Magistrates' Court on 20 October. This was almost a technical procedure to allow the defendant to enter a plea. Notably, by now the three people originally charged, Paraskos, Taylor and Hughes had changed, with only Paraskos remaining in the dock. There is no explanation for this on the public record.

Once the plea was entered the court was

---

[80] *The Guardian*, 21 September 1966, 10

quickly adjourned until December for the full trial. This led to a brief rise in reporting of the case, with *The Liverpool Echo* noting that the charges brought against Paraskos were to be under both the Vagrancy Acts of 1824 and 1837 and the Obscene Publications Act of 1959. Under the Vagrancy Acts Paraskos faced two counts of 'exposing to public view an obscene picture,' and under the Obscene Publications Act a count of 'publishing an obscene article.'[81]

By now the names of the legal teams also emerged. The prosecution was led by Mr G.C. Cox, while the defence in the hands of Harry Waterman. Interestingly, Waterman appears to have attempted to play on what he must have perceived as the magistrate's reluctance to act alone in judging a matter of art. According to the report in *The Huddersfield Daily Examiner*, Waterman suggested that the magistrate may not 'wish to be cast in the role of censor in a matter of art,' and indicated that his client wished to exercise the right to trial by jury. However, the magistrate was clearly not impressed by this argument. He ruled-out trial by jury for the Vagrancy Act charges and left it to

---

[81] *The Liverpool Echo*, 20 October 1966, 20

the prosecution to decide whether the Obscene Publications Act charge should go before a jury. Waterman also set out what would become the main line of defence, that Paraskos's work was serious art, and needed to be judged in the context of the history of art. He stated: 'It is essential that expert evidence should be called so that people who are conversant with the whole history of art can place these pictures into their proper setting.' For this reason the defence would call expert witnesses, including Sir Herbert Read.[82]

Read's involvement in the case is striking. Despite his pre-eminence in the art world, and his well-known views on the freedom of the artist, he was not called upon to give testimony in any of the other trials of writers or artists of this period. His last major intervention in such a case had been in 1944, when he joined a defence committee supporting three anarchist activists accused of inciting sedition in the armed forces by publishing a pacifist poem.[83] To some extent his absence from so many of the censorship trials of the

---

[82] *The Huddersfield Daily Examiner*, 20 October 1966, 1
[83] See David Goodway, *Anarchist Seeds beneath the Snow: Left-Libertarian Thought and British Writers from William Morris to Colin Ward* (Liverpool: Liverpool University Press, 2006) 143-44.

period might have been by choice or even necessity. By 1966 Read was seriously ill with throat cancer, and his public appearances were increasingly rare. This makes his willingness to act as a witness for Paraskos highly unusual.[84]

The trial, presided over by newly-appointed Stipendiary Magistrate John Randolph, with two lay magistrates alongside him, heard Read and the other expert witnesses defend Paraskos's work both in terms of what they considered its essential innocence and on the broader grounds that art possesses license to explore all aspects of human experience, including sex, even when those aspects cannot always be addressed openly in public life. *The Daily Mirror* reported Read telling the court: 'I think to be pornographic a work has to have an intention of that kind. I don't see any sign of that in these pictures.'[85] In *The Guardian* the remark was reported in fuller form: 'To be pornographic, a work has to have an intention of that kind. It has deliberately to pander to perverse instincts. I don't see any sign of

---

[84] Benedict Read and David Thistlewood (eds.), *Herbert Read: A British Vision of World Art* (London: Lund Humphries, 1993) 15
[85] *The Daily Mirror*, 20 December 1966, 10

that in these pictures.'[86] According to *The Liverpool Daily Post*, Read added that he did not think anything that was human and natural could be obscene.[87]

Although this line of defence may have appealed to the art world, and seemed to align with the defence of 'public good' or artistic merit enshrined in the 1959 Obscene Publications Act, it was a poor tactic when set against the early-nineteenth-century attitudes embedded in the Vagrancy Acts. There the central question remained much more prosaic, namely the public nature of the exhibition space. Prosecuting counsel George Cox argued in court that: 'These, in my submission, are matters which in themselves are obscene if they are likely to come before the public, including children, even if they be children of a more adult age.' As reported in *The Daily Mirror*, Cox noted that there was 'no supervision on who went in to see the exhibition.' As a result, the test for the court became 'whether these pictures are likely to deprave or corrupt those who are likely to come into contact with them.'[88]

---

[86] *The Guardian*, 20 December 1966, 3
[87] *The Liverpool Daily Post*, 20 December 1966, 11
[88] *The Daily Mirror*, 20 December 1966, 10

The other defence witnesses largely echoed Read's line. Eric Taylor, Principal of Leeds College of Art, noted that despite almost two-hundred guests attending the private view, no one had complained. On the contrary, there was excitement over the lyrical quality of Paraskos's work. Asked by defence counsel how the paintings differed from a dirty postcard, he replied: 'I feel very strongly about this. A painting or drawing by an artist is entirely different from a lewd photograph.' This prompted the examining magistrate to intervene, asking whether the same image, made by someone who was not an artist, could be considered obscene. Taylor conceded: 'The drawing in the charge could be obscene if not done by an artist. One sees drawings on lavatory walls obviously setting out to be obscene, but this work by a mature artist is not in that category at all.'[89]

Norbert Lynton also argued that art operates outside the everyday reality of our world, stating: 'The whole thing is lifted out of this world: it is very difficult to use this to get any immediate sexual stimulus.'[90]

---

[89] *The Daily Mirror*, 20 December 1966, 10
[90] *The Guardian*, 20 December 1966, 3

A detailed account appeared in the *Nottingham Guardian Journal*, which concentrated on the testimony of John Jones, a lecturer in the Fine Art Department at the University of Leeds. Jones described Paraskos's work as 'gentle, tender, honest, poetic and lyrical.' Asked whether he thought young people might be corrupted by seeing it, Jones replied that he had tried to explain the paintings to his eight-year-old daughter. At this point the magistrate intervened: 'I am not really interested in the views of an eight-year-old child... She doesn't seem to have been given a very accurate description of them.' Jones responded: 'I believe many things in our society stimulate children's sexual thought, and I believe this kind of stimulation is infinitely preferable to many others.' Contrasting Paraskos's images with those found elsewhere in society, he added: 'If (a child) is to have such images in his or her head I would rather them have images of this kind, tenderness, warmth and innocence, than images of another kind.'[91]

The court case lasted two days, ending on 20 December with Paraskos found guilty. Among the papers now held at the National Archives in Kew is a

---

[91] *The Nottingham Guardian Journal*, 21 December 1966, 8

typewritten summary of the proceedings, by an unknown hand. This notes that Paraskos himself was not called to give evidence by either prosecution or defence, on the grounds that 'the test as to whether or not these pictures were obscene was objective and all that the defendant could say was what he himself had intended to convey.' In other words, the court had to decide objectively whether the work was obscene and the manner of its display was unlawful, not whether the artist subjectively believed it to be so. This account also reiterates what we have seen from the press coverage, that the defence 'concentrated upon seeking to show that art would be advanced and be for the public good if these pictures were displayed.'[92]

A summary of the bench's judgement is also preserved. It reads:

> Whilst we appreciate that artists, art critics and experts have properly probably a good deal in common in allowing artists unlimited freedom, and whilst we have sympathy and recognise that standards are advancing and vastly

---

[92] National Archives, Kew, London, DPP2/4193

> different from those of years ago, nevertheless there must be a distinction between liberty and near licence… We have to protect the ordinary member of the public from matters tending to deprave and corrupt. The defence, through these experts, urged that there should be a protection for artists which was not allowed to other less mortals. Clearly this is not so.

The judgement further observed that although expert testimony had been given to claim artistic merit for the work, 'the standpoint of those making that judgement is different from that of the ordinary layman.' From that standpoint, the magistrates decided, the artist was guilty.[93]

More details of the judgement were recorded by *The Daily Telegraph* correspondent, writing that Mr Randolph, giving the decision, said the test was 'simply whether the works displayed could corrupt and deprave those whose minds are open to such immoral influences.' The artist's motivations and intentions were irrelevant. 'He may have the purest and best of

---

[93] National Archives, Kew, London, DPP2/4193

motives,' Randolph explained. 'It may never occur to him that such a painting or drawing had a tendency to deprave or corrupt those whose minds are open to moral influences. That matters not.' He went on to add that whether other artists in the past or present were doing similar things was equally irrelevant.[94]

In the immediate aftermath of the trial there were two main codas that brought an effective end to public discussion of the case in this period. We have already seen Paraskos's own response in his 1967 article for *The Leicester Mercury*, but alongside this should be placed Norbert Lynton's article published in *The Guardian* on 5 January 1967. Paraskos's piece was shot-through with anger, but it was also thoughtful in its diagnosis of the backdoor methods used by those determined to maintain strict control over British culture. In effect, it anticipated by nearly forty years the arguments later advanced by Alan Travis in his history of British censorship, *Bound and Gagged*. Both Paraskos and Travis argued that the legal protections for artistic creation were routinely circumvented by reactionary figures in the police and elsewhere through recourse to

---

[94] *The Daily Telegraph*, 21 December 1966, 11

archaic statutes such as the Vagrancy Acts, or else openly ignored.[95] But *The Leicester Mercury* article is also important within Paraskos's oeuvre for setting him on a lifelong path as a polemicist, frequently writing for the Greek press in Cyprus on art, society and politics.

Lynton's article, by contrast, began with a reminder of the state of the law on obscenity in England at the time, before declaring categorically that the Paraskos case represented a miscarriage of justice. In addition to reiterating the arguments used by the defence in court, Lynton pointed to what he saw as a particular curiosity in the case, namely why Paraskos had been charged when, logically, it should have been the publisher. In this case that would have been either the art school or the owners of the art school and its gallery, namely the City of Leeds itself. That approach would have aligned more closely with the prosecution, also in 1966, of the Robert Fraser Gallery in London, where it was the gallery, not the artist Jim Dine, placed in the dock and found guilty.[96] In highlighting the

---

[95] Alan Travis, *Bound and Gagged: a secret history of obscenity in Britain* (London: Profile Books, 2001) 166f

[96] Norbert Lynton, 'Art and the Expert Witness' in *The Guardian*, 5 January 1967, 7

anomaly of Paraskos being charged as the publisher, Lynton inadvertently draws attention to the unexplained disappearance of Paraskos's co-defendants, Taylor and Hughes, from the prosecution. For Lynton, the likely explanation for all of this was that prosecuting the City of Leeds or its representatives would have been embarrassing for the authorities. But it is difficult not to speculate that another factor was at play. Paraskos was an outsider, an émigré from a former British colony that was, in 1966, frequently in the news due to an ongoing civil war. That status alone may have made him a more vulnerable and convenient target than an art school, entire local authority council, or even his British-born colleagues.

    The Paraskos case does seem to have had an impact on the law. A handwritten note from Ryland Thomas to the Director of Public Prosecutions records that a question was due to be put to the Home Secretary, Roy Jenkins, in the House of Commons on whether the Vagrancy Acts should be amended in light of the case to include an artistic defence. In his response to that question Jenkins stated:

> There is a statutory right for the opinion of experts to be admitted in any proceedings under the Obscene Publications Acts in order to assist the court in deciding whether the publication was justified as being for the public good. There is no similar right in proceedings under the Vagrancy Acts, where the essence of the offence is the wilful exposure of obscene pictures or indecent exhibitions to the public view. I am considering whether any amendment of the law may be desirable.[97]

Lynton was also subsequently asked to give evidence to the Montgomerie Committee, established in 1968 by the Arts Council of Great Britain, to examine reform of Britain's obscenity laws. Drawing heavily on his experience as an expert witness in the Paraskos trial, Lynton reiterated his belief that either the City of Leeds or the art school should have been prosecuted as the publisher, not the artist himself. This prompted committee member Ronald Harwood, of the Writers' Guild of Great Britain, to pose the rhetorical

---

[97] Hansard Commons Debates, 19 January 1967 vol 739 cc111-2W

question, 'was the obscenity in exhibiting a picture, or in painting it?'[98]

Despite Paraskos's claim in *The Leicester Mercury* that accusations of obscenity were a quick and corrupting route for an artist to gain fame, in his case that fame proved short-lived. Apart from a handful of passing references, the case disappeared from the press with remarkable speed, and by the end of 1967 had all but vanished from the media landscape. The last major reference in this period appeared in an editorial in *The Guardian* on 17 January 1970, when Paraskos was cited in connection with the prosecution of the London Art Gallery in Bond Street for showing supposedly obscene images by John Lennon.[99]

Yet there were intimations of this eclipse even before the trial took place. For example, in November 1966, Jasia Reichardt wrote an editorial in *Studio International* which placed the Paraskos trial in a distinctly subsidiary position to the prosecutions of Jim Dine, Hermann Nitsch and the Victorian artist Aubrey

---

[98] Arts Council of Great Britain, *The Obscenity Laws* (London: Andre Deutsch, 1969) 46f
[99] *The Guardian*, 17 January 1970, 10

Beardsley. As those cases took place in London this may have been a simple matter of metropolitan bias, but that bias becomes critically significant when it sidelines a figure who is already marginalised within British society. This represents a clear instance of intersectionality, where multiple, overlapping forms of discrimination converge.[100]

This process of marginalisation was reinforced after the trial. Although Paraskos was invited in 1967 to exhibit at the Institute of Contemporary Arts (ICA) in London, subsequent opportunities exhibit appear to have been few and far between. As far as can be ascertained, not a single review of the ICA show was published, and more telling still, in Anne Massey and Gregor Muir's 2014 book *ICA London 1948–1968*, which purports to list all the exhibitions held at the ICA during this period, the show is omitted altogether.[101]

Even when Paraskos was mentioned in the British press after the trial we get a strong sense of him being dismissed, an effective prelude to marginalisation.

---

[100] Jasia Reichardt, 'Censorship, obscenity and context' in *Studio International*, November 1966, 222-3

[101] Anne Massey and Gregor Muir, *Institute of Contemporary Arts: 1946–1968* (London: Institute of Contemporary Arts, 2014)

Reviewing Paraskos's exhibition in 1970 at the Gallery Caballa in Harrogate for *The Northern Echo*, W. E. Johnson produced what some people might consider a paragon of English superciliousness. Johnson described Paraskos as 'patently self-taught and naïve' and 'like a lesser Chagall.' In relation to the trial four years earlier, Johnson portrayed him as 'an innocent abroad, caught up in something he didn't fully understand.' Moving on to discuss the work on show at the Gallery Caballa, Johnson sounded almost disappointed that it was not more shocking, dismissing it as 'pretty innocent stuff.' Perhaps most revelatory of all Johnson suggested that Herbert Read may have been duped into believing Paraskos was a 'clever artist'.[102]

In making these attacks Johnson repeated many of the tropes used by the British in justifying the continued colonisation of Cyprus. These are exemplified by the book *Bitter Lemons* by the British colonial press officer, and well-known novelist, Lawrence Durrell. Written in the 1950s, Durrell has

---

[102] W.E. Johnson, 'A Second Look at Paraskos' in *The Northern Echo*, 22 May 1970, 7

frequently been accused of viewing the Greeks of Cyprus as little better than children, and at times much worse, in need of the superior guidance of the British colonial authorities.[103] Combining this with Johnson's review of the Paraskos exhibition Harrogate, a pattern emerges in which all Greek Cypriots are seen by the British as naïve, childish and even duplicitous.

After this, mention of the Paraskos trial is very rare. Indeed, even in instances where we might expect it to appear, it seems to be absent. In the case of John A. Walker's exclusion of the Paraskos trial from his 1999 text *Art and Outrage* there was, perhaps, and issue of space being limited.[104] But it is far more perplexing why Paraskos is almost wholly omitted from James Charnley's history of Leeds College of Art, published in 2015. In over 300 pages, Paraskos is mentioned only once, in passing in a list of staff employed at Leeds College of Art by the Head of Fine Art, Eric "Ricky" Atkinson. Even then, Paraskos is only mentioned as part of a quotation of correspondence with Miles

---

[103] See Afroditi Athanasopoulou, 'Durrell in Cyprus: Orientalism and Nationalism in Literary Perspective,' unpublished conference paper (Vancouver, 2014).

[104] John A. Walker *Art and Outrage* (London: Pluto Press, 1999)

McAlinden, former head of first-year students. Inevitably, this means the 1966 obscenity trial is not mentioned at all in Charnley's book, despite the art school's prominent role in what was undoubtedly a prominent legal case.[105] Effectively Paraskos is marginalised by omissions such as this, but the question remains as to why.

Marginalisation is, of course, a common part of the migrant experience, but the nuances of it are revealing. In Derek Horton's review of a retrospective of Paraskos's work held at the Tetley arts centre in Leeds in 2015, which sought to partly recreate the offending 1966 exhibition, we hear strong echoes of the patronising attitudes of earlier writers such as W. E. Johnson towards Paraskos. Like Johnson in 1970, Horton claimed that:

> Paraskos was not himself a radical figure, despite the notoriety surrounding these particular works. His paintings have a naïve charm, influenced by Gauguin, Matisse and

---

[105] James Charnley, *Creative License: From Leeds College of Art to Leeds Polytechnic, 1963-1973* (Cambridge: The Lutterworth Press, 2015) 24

> Fauvism, but do little to test any real
> boundaries of either painterly form or erotic
> content. Their supposedly scandalous nature
> was somewhat exaggerated.[106]

Similarly, Horton acknowledged the paintings had 'naïve charm', but they did 'little to test any real boundaries.' This is an astonishing claim to make given the undeniable fact the British state did determine that these works went beyond acceptable boundaries, to the point of requiring censorship. More than that, the same British state decided in 1966 that it should prosecute a migrant incomer to Britain, as if he were an unwelcome parvenu, with the full force of the law. In dismissing all of this Horton effectively silences the historical dissonance Paraskos introduced, flattening a transgressive act into the safe category of the quirky, charming and inconsequential. As a result, Horton's analysis functions not as a neutral evaluation, but as a

---

[106] Derek Horton, 'Jonathan Trayte: Polyculture / Stass Paraskos: Lovers and Romances' in *Corridor8,* <https://corridor8.co.uk/article/review-jonathan-trayte-polyculture-stass-paraskos-lovers-and-romances-the-tetley-leeds> accessed, 26 August 2025

latter-day reinforcement of the orientalist folkloric trap, and a demonstration of how the 'naïve' label continues to be used to disarm and make invisible the political and conceptual force of non-Western artists.

But if we look at this attitude alongside Charnley's exclusion of the Paraskos trial from his history of Leeds College of Art, we find the emergence of another potential political agenda. In Horton's review Paraskos is compared unfavourably to another Leeds-based artist from the mid-1960s, namely Robin Page. Page was a close friend of Paraskos and, as Horton noted, was the subject of a portrait by Paraskos included in the 2015 Tetley show. Page also features prominently in Charnley's account of Leeds College of Art as an artist who linked the radical pedagogy of Eric Taylor and Harry Thubron in Leeds with emerging conceptual art in 1960s Europe, particularly Fluxus. For both Horton and Charnley, it was Page's performance art that represented the radical and disruptive spirit of 1966, not Paraskos's painting, and one can almost sense their frustration that it was Paraskos who was arrested that year for exhibiting a painting of a nude, rather than Robin Page for his actual nude live-art piece *Merry Christmas '66*.

Alongside these later responses to the Paraskos obscenity trial (or absence of responses in Charnley's case) it is worth setting the monograph written on Paraskos in 2005 by Norbert Lynton. This was the first substantial retelling of the events of the trial since the 1960s. In it Lynton shifted the emphasis in his earlier writings on the trial from arguing it was a miscarriage of justice towards the personal impact it had on Paraskos. He noted that in the end, despite the summoning of expert witnesses and the attempts to explain the nature of art to the three-person bench, it was 'a waste of time.' As he put it: 'The trial must have been a painful experience for (Paraskos): a strange situation in a strange country ... It lives on in Stass's mind.'[107]

This is a sensitive and empathetic understanding of the impact of an event like the trial on an outsider in British society. A Jewish refugee, who arrived in Britain after fleeing Nazi Germany in 1938, it is tempting to see this empathy for the outsider facing

---

[107] Norbert Lynton, *Stass Paraskos* (London: Orage Press, 2003) 18f

agents of the state as arising from Lynton's own early experiences.[108] Certainly it is an attitude in marked contrast to those of Johnson in 1970 and Horton in 2015. Lynton's book drew in part on interviews with Paraskos conducted in Cyprus in 2002 and 2003, following his return to the island in 1989. It is therefore reasonable to assume that Lynton's sombre assessment was shaped by Paraskos himself. In 1966 Paraskos had every reason to fear prosecution, much as any migrant arriving in Britain today might, since contact with the police and legal system can elicit fear and foreboding in those who have recently settled in a new country.

The Cyprus background is also important. When Paraskos left the island in the mid-1950s it was in the grip of an armed insurgency led by EOKA militants seeking to end British colonial rule. This brutal conflict only ended in 1959 with Britain's near-unilateral decision to make Cyprus an independent republic. In the five years leading up to independence, attacks on British military personnel, and sometimes on non-military residents, were a regular occurrence.

[108] M.G. McNay, Obituary to Norbert Lynton in *The Guardian*, 3 November 2007

British soldiers nicknamed the main shopping street in the capital, Nicosia, 'murder mile', while ambushes were common in the countryside.[109] British forces also conducted raids on suspected EOKA hideouts, including one in the village of Vavla in 1958, during which the poet and EOKA fighter Michael Parides, a cousin of Paraskos, was killed. A monument to him now stands outside the archaeological museum in Larnaca.

In the complex politics of Cyprus, however, it was not the right-wing nationalism of EOKA that appealed to Paraskos, but the island's communist party, AKEL, which he joined as a teenager. AKEL too was banned by the British colonial authorities, meaning contact with the police or judiciary, even in Britain, must surely have carried intimidating connotations. Again, this is something those who might blithely

---

[109] See Carl Warner, *Emergency Exits: IWM Photography Collection* (London: Imperial War Museum, 2025)

dismiss the trial as 'a rather parochial case'[110] are likely to miss.

In bringing these three accounts of Leeds in the 1960s together — Lynton, Horton and Charnley — the lens provided by Hayden White is again useful in revealing the possible hidden motivations. According to White, the meaning of an historical account lies not simply in the facts it presents but in the kind of story into which those facts are organised. Historians (or critics), such as Lynton, Charnley and Horton, shape the material they face by structuring it in accordance with an archetypal narrative form, a process White called emplotment. White identified four principal modes of emplotment, romance, tragedy, comedy and satire, each with its own conventions for giving coherence and meaning to events. The story of Paraskos and the Paraskos trial might thus be emplotted as a tragedy in which we see the persecution of a migrant newly arrived in Britain. Alternatively it might

---

[110] Derek Horton, 'Jonathan Trayte: Polyculture / Stass Paraskos: Lovers and Romances' in *Corridor8*, <https://corridor8.co.uk/article/review-jonathan-trayte-polyculture-stass-paraskos-lovers-and-romances-the-tetley-leeds> accessed, 26 August 2025

be emplotted as a comedy in which prudish magistrates are unable to distinguish art from pornography. Or it might be seen as a romance in which an heroic artist is initially persecuted but later vindicated. Whatever archetypal structure is selected, we can see in this case that the emplotment of the Paraskos story by Lynton is very different to its employment by Horton, even though both were faced with the same material evidence. What this demonstrates is that the choice of one narrative plot or structure over another is never neutral. It is a political act, that encourages the reader to see a story in a particular way.

Although White was scrupulously careful to stress that emplotment is not necessarily evidence of a consciously held ideological position, clearly it can be. But even if the emplotment is an unconscious act, it always has ideological implications shaping the moral and political significance of the story being told. Consequently we can see that Paraskos could not be the avant-garde hero in a romantic tale for Horton. That role could only be reserved for an artist like Robin Page. As a result Paraskos is cast instead as a false hero whose mendacity as an avant-garde artist must be exposed to allow the true hero to emerge.

By the same token, Charnley's emplotment of the history of Leeds College of Art as the story of an avant-garde art school also requires a figure like Page to take the central role as the romantic lead. Initially mocked, marginalised and misunderstood, it is Page who is ultimately vindicated by Charnley as the true representative of progressive modernism in this period. For that to happen Paraskos must be marginalised to the point of silence through outright omission. In this act of emplotment, the silencing of Paraskos is not an accident or a mere personal perspective, it is a narrative necessity and a deliberate act.

As this demonstrates, emplotment needs to be understood as part of an effort to construct a canonical story of this period in British cultural history. In this context feminist and post-colonial readings on the construction of canonical art history are particularly instructive. For example, Seodial Deena notes that the Western canon is not simply constructed by active inclusion of some narratives over others, it also requires the active silencing of non-canonical narratives. The canon 'maintains silencing by an effort to maintain males, especially white males, at the centre of literary and critical discussions,' Deena writes. 'They have always occupied the centre, and central occupation has denied them the understanding and compassion necessary for empathy with the marginalised.' Citing Barbara T. Christian, Deena notes that the canon secures itself by keeping the normative white Western men at the centre, and in that context the presence of non-normative figures becomes a threat to its integrity.[111] It is a process that Pierre Bourdieu might describe as a structural exclusion masked as historical neutrality.[112]

There is no doubt that Paraskos can be read in this light, as a threat to a Western avant-gardist narrative as it manifested itself in Leeds, that struggled to accept him at the time of the trial, and continues to struggle to assimilate him now. This struggle is only partly rooted in his intellectual and aesthetic orientation, as the tone in which he has been discussed

---

[111] Seodial Deena, "Colonial and Canonical Marginalisation and Oppression on the Basis of Gender', in *CLA Journal,* vol. 40, no. 1, 1996, 57-8
[112] See Pierre Bourdieu, *The Rules of Art: Genesis and Structure of the Literary Field* (Cambridge: Polity Press, 1996) 47–55

suggests very strongly that it is also rooted in a Western orientalist view of his non-Western origins. In a very real sense there is a paradoxical alignment between the reactionary state that prosecuted Paraskos in 1966 on one side, and the self-appointed guardians of the history of avant-garde rebellion of that time on the other. Both work, in different ways, to exclude him, but the effect is the same. While he was censored directly by the criminal justice system over five decades ago, he has also been silenced through neo-orientalist assertions of his naïvety, parochialism and child-like innocence, in a process of marginalisation that appears still to be active today.

Chapter 4:
Song to the Siren:
collective making with the refuse of Capitalism

The Great Wall of Lempa is a sprawling, eclectic mix of materials and forms, ranging from cement blocks and wine bottles to large hands and abstract shapes in coloured plaster. It is a dynamic artwork that creates a physical and metaphorical boundary between the artistic space of the former art school founded by Stass Paraskos, in the village of Lempa, and the sublunary space outside. In a sense it is a barrier to the inartistic and anti-artistic forces that threaten to overwhelm places like the Cyprus College of Art — forces that did in fact succeed in destroying it in 2025 — and a marker to anyone passing through the iron gate in the wall that they are entering into a different kind of reality.

  Norbert Lynton encapsulated the spirit of the wall in his 2005 monograph on Paraskos, noting it was 'a major exercise in recycling,' integrating discarded materials, students' sculptures, and found objects into a playful and unpredictable ensemble. Lynton vividly described the wall's surrealist spirit, contrasting it with the nightmare visions of Salvador Dalí and instead likening it to the whimsical creations of Joan Miró. He observed, 'Like nature, it lives,' capturing the wall's romantic, evolving and organic quality.[113]

This romantic aspect to the wall was important to Paraskos but, as we shall see, the wall can also be understood through ideas of self-definition and self-mythologisation. It can be read as a kind of autobiographical form of emplotment. Its growth was in itself a narrative process, an unfolding story told by Paraskos and others to mark the Cyprus College of Art as distinct from any other art school, not only in Cyprus but internationally.

Of course, the association of art schools with distinctive physical forms has a long history. Charles Rennie Mackintosh's 1897 Art Nouveau building for the Glasgow School of Art, for example, embodied his principles of good design in its structure, with the aim of providing inspiration for students. Henry van de Velde pursued a similar vision in his 1905 Arts and

---

[113] Norbert Lynton, *Stass Paraskos* (London: Orage Press, 2003) 91

Crafts-inspired buildings for what would become the Bauhaus in Weimar. And most famous of all are the iconic Bauhaus buildings at Dessau, in which Walter Gropius translated the Bauhaus art school's aesthetic and philosophical beliefs into a functional modernist architecture, again designed to shape the attitudes of the students. In each case, the building acted as a material manifesto, embedding aesthetic principles into the institution itself and providing a narrative framework for the education offered there. To borrow Hayden White's term, and use it in ways he would undoubtedly reject, these buildings were acts of emplotment, the organisation of meaning through form.

The Great Wall of Lempa was arguably a comparable act of emplotment, and like the examples from Glasgow, Weimar and Dessau it too shifted the concept of narrative employment from written to material form. It exemplified what might be called a material narrative, the inscription of story, ethos and myth into physical form, where meaning is produced not only through words but the embodied, evolving presence of the wall itself.

In structural terms, the Great Wall of Lempa was less a two-dimensional barrier than a sprawling three-dimensional sculpture that spilled outward onto the road as well as inward, into the former art school's yard. Constructed primarily of hand-moulded concrete, into which were embedded fragments of discarded pottery and domestic tiles, its main body rose to around two metres in height. The forms were organic and predominantly abstract, but growths and extensions projected outwards that were figurative. This included a bright yellow donkey, seated in front of the wall on the edge of the road, a woman in traditional Cypriot dress, and a large gorilla, encrusted with mosaic-like fragments of white bathroom tiles. Above all this, was set a figure on a bicycle, cut from thin sheet metal that had once been an advertising sign for Carlsberg Beer, and next to this was an actual concrete mixer, referencing playfully the origin of the main building material of the wall.

Around these objects were various semi-abstract figures, most looking out, carefully watching the gate for intruders, while all over the wall were embedded glass beer and wine bottles, both decorative in themselves, but also like eyes for the wall itself, to look out for trouble. More mischievously, they may have alluded to the fondness of some of the art school's students for drink.

Emplotment necessarily requires a narrative form, and that narrative was embodied in the wall as it grew and evolved over time. Beyond the figures keeping watch, and the wall itself having glass-bottle eyes, many elements evoked Cyprus's troubled history. A human figure, also cut from sheet metal, peered from behind rusty iron bars, the corrosion implying a long incarceration. Around him stood oil drums, filled with concrete and painted in bright colours, recalling the makeshift oil-drum fortifications of the Green Line military lookouts in central Nicosia. High in one corner loomed the colossal gorilla, overlooking it all. Often read as playful, the gorilla was in reality a deeply ambiguous and potentially threatening figure. The fact it sat on top of a dry public well, created by the British during their colonial rule of Cyprus, fed into the ambiguity of its narrative, as the British colonial authorities who brought clean drinking water to the village, could also be brutal in their response to dissent.

The colonial reading of this element of the wall, was perhaps reinforced by the gorilla's companion, the figure of a crusader knight emblazoned with red crosses, possibly meant to evoke the English king, Richard the Lionheart, who briefly ruled Cyprus in the middle ages. All of this implied the gorilla may be calm for the moment, but it remained an ominous presence.

This suggests that while the emplotment of the wall related to the wider history of Cyprus, it also needs to be considered in relation to the specific history of the village of Lempa in which the wall once stood. In that context the narrative can be seen to take on the form of a resurrection story, a cycle of death and renewal. Lempa had been a Turkish-Cypriot village until intercommunal violence in 1963 forced its inhabitants to flee. In the two decades that followed, the village almost disappeared, its small mud-brick houses crumbling rapidly without the constant maintenance of their owners. In 1974, a handful of Greek refugees displaced from the north of Cyprus after the Turkish invasion renovated five or six dwellings, but this tiny community, whose members were desperate to return to their own homes, cannot be seen as a re-founding of the community. In many ways, Lempa remained a dead village.

It was only with the arrival of Paraskos and the Cyprus College of Art in 1981 that renewal began in earnest. After the loss of Famagusta to the Turkish invasion, Paraskos relocated the Cyprus College of Art to Kato Paphos, but by the 1980s it too was invaded, albeit by tourists whose interests were widely different to those of an art school. As a result, Paraskos began his search for an alternative site, and Lempa, with its abandoned houses, seemed ideal. With state support, the old school building was restored as studios and four village houses rebuilt as accommodation. The Government of Cyprus declared that Lempa would be the College's forever home.

Even today, Lempa retains a semi-rural atmosphere, perched above a perpetually green valley, watered by a beck that flows even in the driest summers. Yet this beauty exists only because of violence. Had Lempa been a Greek-Cypriot village, its fields would have been built on long ago, much as the two neighbouring Greek villages of Chlorakas and Kissonerga have been developed. But Lempa, or

Lemba as it was originally called, was a Turkish-Cypriot community, and its owners Turkish Cypriots. They still own the land, which is frozen in time and largely unused. That is why, in Lempa, it is important to remember that violence has led to survival, and this cruel paradox made Lempa a fertile space for a work of public art like the Great Wall of Lempa. The village is a liminal zone, caught not only between an older Cyprus of unspoiled landscapes and ancient traditions and a new Cyprus of hyper-commercialised tourism, but between a place that is both enchanted with the peace of nature and scarred by the violence of humankind. As a result, the wall's narrative of watchfulness, threat and survival can be seen as an emplotment of the narrative of Lempa itself.

In writing this I accept that my interpretation of the symbolic meaning of the wall may be unduly negative. For Norbert Lynton it was a far more joyful creation. He described the wall as a creation with 'Fun, little joys, big jokes, and here and there a weird or scary form… encountered in what threatens to become a sort of linear art jungle, a monument to human ways of making things grow in what is still very much nature's world.'[114] Yet, as Iakovos Aristidou, the former Director General of the Ministry of Education, has observed, the creation of the Cyprus College of Art was never easy and so we might speculate the humour in the wall was of the biting kind. Aristidou recalled Paraskos's own words, noting that he wanted to create 'an environment and tradition of artistic creativity in our homeland,' despite facing overt and covert hostility in sections of the civil service.[115]

Paraskos's own view of the Great Wall of Lempa was expressed in ways that veered between extreme pragmatism and equally extreme romanticism. Describing the origins of the wall in disarmingly simple terms, he stated: 'Originally there was no wall separating the street from our yard. And we thought we'd build the wall. So we started building a new wall.' Using debris left by students, including rejected sculptures, he began arranging the fragments into rhythms and juxtapositions that transcended their

---

[114] Norbert Lynton, *Stass Paraskos* (London: Orage Press, 2003) 91
[115] Ιακωβος Αριστείδου, "Ο Στας Παράσκος και η Λέμπα," in *Simerini*, 4 February, 2020,
http://simerini.sigmalive.com/article/2020/2/4/o-stas-paraskos-kai-e-lempa/

practical function. 'What was originally meant as a wall started becoming a work of art,' he reflected. What had begun as necessity evolved into a process of discovery, where artistic instinct transformed discarded refuse into artistic form. With that process the wall soon developed into something more than a pragmatic division of the College yard from the road. 'We thought we'd keep doing this in an open-ended way,' Paraskos said, imagining the Cyprus College of Art would one day be swallowed up entirely by the wall. This romantic ideal, to transform a place of teaching art into a living, breathing work of art, underscores the deeply personal and utopian character of the project. As Paraskos put it: 'It's a... romantic way to finish a college of art, to transform it into a work of art.'[116]

It is important to note that the collective pronoun 'we' used by Paraskos in discussing the sculpture wall was not an affectation. It reflected the communal nature of the wall's creation. Much of the material of the wall came from discarded waste, including sculptural fragments produced by students and visiting artists at the College. This made the Great

---

[116] See Appendix B.

Wall of Lempa a communal act. A photograph in the Paraskos family archive shows Paraskos's wife, Mary, moving boulders onto the concrete plinth from which the wall grew, at the very beginning of the process of creating the sculpture wall, an image that underlines how the work was constructed by many hands, and demonstrating how Paraskos often acted less as sole fabricator than as *chef d'orchestre*, directing, encouraging, and integrating the efforts of others. Another photograph, probably from 1988, also preserved in the family archive, shows Paraskos with artists Tony Hayward and Bob Stone, alongside students from the College, collaborating on forming the giant hand that thrusts out from the wall into the adjacent street.

By 2005 the wall had grown to a height of two-and-a-half metres, but even then it continued to absorb new contributions. This included a double plaster column, probably the most overtly surrealist element in appearance, painted in bright yellow household paint. This was created by artists Evelyn Bennett and Chris Rutter on their first stay at the Cyprus College of Art as visiting artists. Their participation in the creation of the wall creates an interesting double-take, as they work together as a single artistic voice, and in this context their own collaboration is grafted onto a much larger one.

The layering of different makers, materials and memories reinforces the wall's status as a collective narrative in material form, a palimpsest of many hands. But this collaborative ethos was not an isolated phenomenon in Paraskos's career. In the early 2000s Paraskos and fellow Cypriot artist Stelios Votsis experimented with joint paintings in which each worked on the same canvas, but in their own distinct styles. Unlike the hierarchical model of the Old Masters or modern sculptors such as Rodin and Moore, where assistants suppressed their individuality to serve a master's vision, the works of Paraskos and Votsis allowed each artist to remain a distinct and identifiable voice. Later, the self-taught artist Stefos Metaxas joined them, creating paintings with three readily identifiable authors in a process Paraskos himself described as being inspired by anarchist theory.[117]

---

[117] See Μιχάλης Παρασκός, *Οι Αναρχικού* (Λευκωσία: Βούλα Κονικίου Λτδ, 2007) 1-2

The Great Wall of Lempa can be viewed as prefiguring this experiment. Constructed from discarded materials and contributions by students, visiting artists and family members, the wall functioned less as a monument to possibly outmoded notions of individual genius than as a collective emplotment of community. In this the wall can be said to have both reflected the fractured histories of Lempa and Cyprus, and offered the enixa of amelioration. The fragments of which the wall was made were broken and discarded, but through the wall they were integrated into a new rhythm, forming a coherent if unpredictable whole. Like the collaborative canvases, the wall represented a shared space subject to negotiated coexistence, where multiple hands and voices were able to resist subsumption. We can read the Great Wall of Lempa as a collective reconciling image, reintegrating and reconciling the fractured history of Lempa as a community into a new whole.

The political aspect of this is paramount. In *The Aesthetic Dimension* Herbert Marcuse argued that art can negate existing social realities and through its autonomy gesture toward alternative modes of being.

From this perspective the Great Wall of Lempa can seen not simply as a collection of eccentric bricolage, or some amusing backdrop for tourists to take selfies, but as a utopian gesture of resistance to capitalism and the fragmentation it induces in society.[118]

This collective authorship and open-ended form also resonates with Nicolas Bourriaud's account of relational aesthetics. Writing in the 1990s, Bourriaud argued that contemporary art is increasingly defined not by the production of discrete objects but by the creation of social interstices, spaces of encounter and exchange. This posits art as 'a state of encounter' rather than a finished work.[119] Constructed over decades by students, artists, and family members, it is not difficult to see the Great Wall of Lempa in these terms. It was created less as a closed artwork, with a definitive moment of completion, than as an ongoing process of collaboration. Its relationship to the art school that it surrounded, and the unpredictable stages that moved it forward, means that its physical form provided a stage

---

[118] Herbert Marcuse, *The Aesthetic Dimension: Toward a Critique of Marxist Aesthetics* (Boston: Beacon Press, 1978) 6

[119] Nicolas Bourriaud, *Relational Aesthetics*, trans. Simon Pleasance and Fronza Woods (Dijon: Les presses du réel, 2002) 18

for collective action, a process of moving stones, embedding fragments, tiling surfaces and so on, and its presence offered a site for gathering, discussion and imaginative projection. In essence, like the collaborative canvases of Paraskos, Votsis and Metaxas, the Great Wall of Lempa was a shared space in which difference was not erased but negotiated.

This aspect of Bourriaud suggests the Great Wall of Lempa can be seen as having been a work of art that was almost performative in its nature, eliciting multiple vital and kinetic interactions, so that we have the seemingly paradoxical situation in which something as seemingly solid and permanent as a wall, made from stone, plaster, wood, clay and concrete, was also ephemeral in the way its forms changed over time as new people participated in its construction. Indeed, it is possible to see the wall not as an art object at all, but as having been an art process, or a kind of long term Happening, more aligned with the performance work of Paraskos's friend Robin Page and the Fluxus artists than traditional works of art. This makes me wonder whether, when we hear Paraskos say he did not think the wall would ever be finished,[120] we should not think of that statement as the mournful cry of an artist who does not think he will live long enough to see his work reach its end. Rather it is a conceptual statement to say this work of art has no final end point. As a performative act it must continually grow and evolve, like a living thing in motion, or else it is dead. Returning to Bourriaud's notion of relational aesthetics it is arguable that the value of the Great Wall of Lempa lay less in a hypothetical finished form, than in its existence as an ongoing event, an intersubjective space opened up by Paraskos for students, artists and visitors.[121]

    Taking the idea of the Great Wall of Lempa as an eternal work of performance art, it is useful to see it in relation to the ideas of Peggy Phelan. Phelan argues that performance's only life is in the present time and that it 'becomes itself through disappearance'.[122] From this we can argue that the Great Wall of Lempa's truest

---

[120] See Appendix B

[121] Nicolas Bourriaud, *Relational Aesthetics*, trans. Simon Pleasance and Fronza Woods (Dijon: Les presses du réel, 2002) 18

[122] Peggy Phelan, *Unmarked: The Politics of Performance* (London: Routledge, 1993) 146-7

ontology lies less in its manifestation as a physical form than in the unrepeatable acts that made it, and in how those acts inevitably slip into memory. Phelan's account of performance as disappearance deepens this reading. For Phelan, performance exists in the moment and vanishes as it occurs, resisting 'the colonialist/imperialist appetite for possession.'[123] Surely the construction of the wall was performative in precisely this sense, the carrying of stones, the embedding of bottles (having drunk their contents!), the improvisation of forms and so on, were all ephemeral acts, unrepeatable and uncommodifiable, but essential to the creative act. What endures is a material trace, but that is no more than a vestige of vanished performances. If Bourriaud stresses relational encounters and Phelan ephemeral acts, what we might suggest is that the Great Wall of Lempa shows how both can be sedimented into matter, resulting in a semi-permanent structure that nonetheless bears witness to the performative processes of its making.

---

[123] Peggy Phelan, *Unmarked: The Politics of Performance* (London: Routledge, 1993) 6-7

This also helps us to conceptualise the curious ambiguities the wall threw up. The wall was joyful, funny and fun, but at the same time the wall was anxious, wary and watchful. In some places it was rude, as with the art critic depicted as an exclaiming ass, and in other places it was tender, as with the much-loved image in Cyprus of the mother and child. It formed a barrier to the road and the outside world it led to, and yet it spilled out onto that road, even offering a giant hand of friendship. The wall was, in effect, mercurial, moving between different points of meaning as a dancer might move through different movements in an improvised performance. As a result, the wall can be seen as a kind of dance through time and in that dance it appears to have offered itself up as a corrective to the linear utilitarianism and hostile brutality of the world outside. The wall was in effect a carnivalesque riposte to a world of throwaway meanings, people and things. In both a literal and a metaphorical sense, it offered those things discarded by capitalism a place of refuge in which they could, for a short while at least, regain value and meaning. It is no wonder the only written sign on the wall itself was the anarchist circle-A, as the wall can be conceptualised as having been an anarchist commune as much as the three-artist paintings of Paraksos, Votsis and Metaxas were anarchist communes.

    Theorising the wall in this way draws out a number of possible readings, but that cannot hide the paradoxical position of the main actors in the emplotment we have described. These were Paraskos, the wall (and by extension the Cyprus College of Art) and the geographical location of these in both Lempa and Cyprus. Paraskos clearly had avant-garde ambitions with the wall, drawing on romantic plot forms to describe it as 'a significant work of art' which would one day be recognised as such. A decade after his death, as the wall seems to be in a state of terminal decay following the government's eviction of its caretaker, the Cyprus College of Art, from the site in Lempa, we might argue we are still waiting for that day to come. The emplotment trope Paraskos employed in relation to the wall was romantic in the sense that it relied on the romantic hero, the wall, being ignored or scorned, before rising triumphant to be recognised as the great work of art Paraskos claimed it to be.

Globally-renowned critics such as Lynton interpreted the wall through a modernist lens, likening it to the playful surrealism of Miró or the immersive environments of Gaudí and Rodia. Yet locally, the wall was often treated as eccentric bricolage, a curiosity for tourists, a backdrop for photographs, or even an eyesore. Successive Cypriot governments have largely ignored it, culminating in the closure of the Cyprus College of Art in Lempa in 2025, which underscored its vulnerability to bureaucratic hostility. As a result the future of the Great Wall of Lempa might not lie in its physical endurance but in its transformation into memory and myth, a trajectory that recalls Phelan's claim that performance 'becomes itself through disappearance.'[124] Phelan notes that live acts 'clog the smooth machinery of reproductive representation necessary to the circulation of capital,' which is precisely why they draw censure. The wall's refusal of commodity form positions it as fiscally and ideologically illegible to bureaucratic reason. Indeed, the wall's ambiguous reception, admired, ignored or derided, is

---

[124] Peggy Phelan, *Unmarked: The Politics of Performance* (London: Routledge, 1993) 146

itself part of its material narrative. Whether conserved or lost, the wall is legible through what Phelan calls 'representation without reproduction.' Its presence survives as a choreography of remembered acts, stories, descriptions and returns to the site, which re-stage rather than replace what has disappeared.[125]

---

[125] Peggy Phelan, *Unmarked: The Politics of Performance* (London: Routledge, 1993) 148-9

Chapter 5:
I Am What I Am:
narrating the self

In this chapter I want to look at a diary that Stass Paraskos kept in the summer of 1968 during a visit to Cyprus. In doing so I want to suggest that the diary is not merely a record of events but a multi-layered work that functions simultaneously as a performative literary text, the inaugural artwork of the Cyprus College of Art and as a potent document of post-colonial cultural assertion.

Although the diary is reproduced in full in my earlier book, *In Search of Sixpence*, I have also included it in this volume as an appendix.[126]

In the summer of 1968 Stass Paraskos visited Cyprus, staying in Larnaca, the nearest large town to his village of birth, called Anaphotia. Accompanying him was his family, comprising his wife Mary and four children, Stanley, Margaret, Paul and Christopher. Also with them was the Leeds-based poet, Martin Bell, and

---

[126] See Appendix A.

his partner, Christine McCausland. The group had travelled overland, by train through mainland Europe to the port of Brindisi in Italy, and from there by ferry-boat to Cyprus.

Despite the lavish-sounding journey, this was not a well-financed trip and by the time the group reached Cyprus money was desperately low. Paraskos was relying on hoped-for sales from an exhibition of his work being held at the Hilton Hotel in the capital of Cyprus, Nicosia, and Bell on the promise of a bursary for the trip from the Arts Council of Great Britain. This had been provided on the basis of it forming a future book of anecdotes and poems.[127] That book never appeared, although Bell wrote some of his most evocative poems during the visit.[128] More relevant to this study, Paraskos also began writing about the trip, producing a prose diary of the group's adventures as they attempted to gain an audience with the first president of the still newly-created Republic of Cyprus, President Archbishop Makarios. Their aim was to elicit

---

[127] See report in *The Leicester Mercury*, 22 October 1968, 7
[128] Martin Bell, *Complete Poems*, ed. Peter Porter (Newcastle upon Tyne: Bloodaxe Books, 1988)

his support to start the first art school in Cyprus, an institution that would go on to become the Cyprus College of Art.

The diary is a curious text. It appears to operate as a factual record of events, but if it is factual it is deeply problematic. The most significant problem comes from the original manuscript itself which appears to have written corrections added in a different hand to Paraskos. This might make us want to see the diary as a work of art, fabricated and edited from life, rather than a simple record of events. If this is the case we might also wonder if the diary is in fact a political document, designed to emplot the founding of the Cyprus College of Art as a romantic act in which there is an idealistic aim, numerous setbacks and a final triumph over adversity. At the very least these clear signs of editing suggest the diary is a performative act, as much designed to be seen, even if it was never actually published, as it was intended to record events for personal recollection.

To a certain extent this involves a form of teleological reasoning that would no doubt offend those wedded to a more pedantic historical approach in

which effect follows cause. I can justify this only by an
appeal to Koselleckian principles, according to which
the 1968 diary might not function as a plan or blueprint
for the Great Wall of Lempa, but rather as a future-
oriented horizon of expectation whose meaning
becomes fully legible only once the wall enters the space
of experience in the 1980s.[129] While the wall does not
fulfil an intention set out in or by the diary, it
nonetheless retrospectively constitutes the diary as its
point of origin.

This reading offers a neat exegesis, suggesting
that the Cyprus College of Art and its surrounding
sculpture wall were, from the outset, oriented toward
becoming a work of art rather than an institution in
which people might study in order to gain diplomas.
Such an interpretation undoubtedly transforms a

---

[129] Reinhart Koselleck's distinction between *Erfahrungsraum* (space of experience) and *Erwartungshorizont* (horizon of expectation) provides a useful framework for this reading. Koselleck argues that in modern historical consciousness the horizon of expectation increasingly exceeds accumulated experience, with the result that earlier moments may acquire their full historical meaning only retrospectively. Later developments do not therefore fulfil prior intentions so much as constitute earlier moments as points of origin after the fact. See Reinhart Koselleck, *Futures Past: On the Semantics of Historical Time*, trans. Keith Tribe (New York: Columbia University Press, 2004) 255–275

record of ephemeral experiences, social relations, and political contingencies into a narrative of origin. Yet it also suggests that, far from being merely haphazard or *ad hoc*, as the College is sometimes portrayed, there existed from the very beginning a consistent creative hypothesis underpinning the Cyprus College of Art. Read in this way, it can be understood as a near six-decade-long act of conceptual performance art.

The Paraskos diary itself is an unassuming object. Comprising a wire-spiral-bound reporters' notebook, approximately 20 cm tall and 12 cm wide, it might easily have become a cheap throwaway artefact, intended for ephemeral notes rather than a record for posterity. Paraskos's handwriting is easily legible, the way he formed letters almost childlike, and the whole text is written in blue biro pen ink. In all of this it is notable how unlike a diary the document appears, to the extent it might be considered less a diary in the sense of a journal, and more a way to keep notes for the promised, but never delivered, book commissioned by the Arts Council of Great Britain. This raises a fundamental question as to what is a diary.

Philippe Lejeune is a key theorist who has tried to pin down what we mean when we describe something as a diary. In *The Practice of the Private Journal* (2009) he begins with the most basic definition, a diary is written in dated instalments. Each entry is usually self-contained but linked to the others through a linear chronology. This gives the diary a discontinuous, fragmentary form, rather than the coherent narrative arc we expect from literary fiction or history. It is the antithesis of the Aristotelian notion of a narrative with a beginning, a middle and an end. Lejeune describes this as 'writing in pieces, day after day, without knowing where it will lead.'[130]

All of these features seem to fit the Paraskos diary. The reader senses throughout that neither the attempt to meet President Makarios, nor the diary project itself, may reach a satisfying resolution. As Lejeune notes, diaries by their very nature have no preordained ending as each entry looks forward to the next day, but without the guarantee of continuation.

---

[130] Philippe Lejeune, 'The Diary as "Antifiction,"' in Jeremy D. Popkin and Julie Rakow (eds.), *On Diary* (Honolulu: University of Hawaii Press, 2009) 183

Yet the Paraskos diary diverges from this model in one crucial respect. It does reach what appears to be a providential ending in that the meeting with Makarios does take place. Essentially it has an Aristotelian structure. There is even a moral commentary attached at the end, when Paraskos delights in the reversal of fortune against neighbours who had derided him and Bell as beatniks. 'Who's the beatnik now?' he asks rhetorically.

While Paraskos's text shares many features of the diary form as defined by Lejeune, this structural dénouement seems to fail the test Lejeune sets for a diary. Rather than remaining open-ended and fragmentary, it imposes precisely the kind of closure, the providential ending, that the diary form is supposed to resist.

Jochen Hellbeck can perhaps help us to understand this conundrum. In *Diaries Between Literature and History,* Hellbeck argues that the diary straddles multiple compositional genres, being both historical by recollecting daily events, but also aesthetic and even artful in a literary sense. While we might dispute any claim for actual objectivity in academic history writing, recognising the emplotment of history and selection of events is a subjective selection process, in a diary, like the novel, there is never any true claim for objectivity.[131]

In the Paraskos diary we are given a range of fragmentary anecdotes. This includes references to Bell's frequent drunkenness:

> **22nd August 1968:** I went to the beach with the family. An hour later Christine came to remind me of an arrangement I had with Martin to go to town to see if the money from the Arts Council had arrived. Martin also needed some shoes, and to send telegrams to Charles Osborne and Peter Porter. Martin was supposed to be waiting for me on the steps of my house, but he was not there so I went to his place and found him lying on his bed stone drunk. He must have drunk a bottle of brandy in the half hour between Christine leaving him and my arrival.

---

[131] Jochen Hellbeck, 'The Diary between Literature and History: A Historian's Critical Response,' in *The Russian Review* 63, no. 4 (October 2004) 621

Also there are insults from their neighbours in Larnaca:

> **7th September 1968:** The comments of some of our neighbours in Larnaca have not always being kind. At Xenou's a woman said, 'I did not see her clean her house in two months,' about Christine. 'And you can smell ouzo when you pass by on the street.' Another neighbour stopped me in the bank and said, 'Your wife allows the children to wander anywhere they like. I suppose that's how Englishwomen bring up their children.'

And even commentary on Paraskos's sense of embarrassment at the behaviour of his own children:

> Our friend's elderly mother was also ill and kept going to bed for a little rest every half hour or so. Our arrival clearly did not make things easier for them. Our kids are noisy and very curious with other people's property. Coffee was spilt, cakes and biscuits eaten, and

> antique plates were broken. When Christine
> informed everybody that the toilet was broken I
> felt ashamed and offered to try and fix it.

All of this might seem trivial, but they are in fact the subjective texture of Cyprus as seen by Paraskos in the summer of 1968, each caught somewhere between the reality of the events happening and the subjective response of Paraskos experiencing them.

This tallies with the views of Irina Paperno. In *What Can Be Done with Diaries?*, she suggests that when reading what purports to be a diary there is a kind of game played between writer and reader. The writer presents themselves as sincere and honest, creating a 'contract of sincerity' to which the reader implicitly agrees. The mechanisms for this contract are embedded in the diaristic form itself, in the daily instalments, dated entries and a first-person voice all promising intimate honesty, both in terms of events and commentary.[132] This opens the possibility of playful literary uses of the diary. Anna Jameson's *The Diary of an Ennuyée* (1826), for

---

[132] Irina Paperno, *Stories of the Soviet Experience: Memoirs, Diaries, Dreams* (Ithaca: Cornell University Press, 2009) 10

example, invites us to sign up to the contract of sincerity even though it is an entirely fictional diary. In such cases the sincerity is performative rather than factual.

For Paperno the authenticity of any diary is essentially performative, generated by the form itself rather than by accuracy of reference. As such, the diary functions as a literary device, not unlike Hayden White's notion of emplotment, and offers no guarantee of factual truth. The Paraskos diary demonstrates this paradox clearly. Its tone invites us to accept it as a candid record of Cyprus in 1968, yet the visible signs of editing and the imposition of a providential ending undermine any simple claim to truth. In life there are rarely providential endings. It is precisely because the diary appears to be transparent that it gains rhetorical power, but this apparent transparency conceals its constructed nature and the mythologising project it enacts.

A useful parallel here is provided by Herbert Read's 1933 text *The Innocent Eye* in which we can see similar traits to those identified by Lejeune, Hellbeck, and Paperno. Although presented as a memoir of childhood in rural Ryedale, rather than a diary, it has many of the identifying qualities of a diary, being a personal account of events seen at first hand and commentary on them. Even so, it is less a record of raw memory than the shaping of fragments into a romanticised life narrative. Read selected and aestheticised moments of childhood, such as the sight of fields, the discovery of books and the play of light, so that they became symbolic episodes rather than neutral recollections. In doing so he turned the discontinuity of remembered real-life experiences into a form of romantic myth, an 'innocent eye' that retrospectively framed his later vocation as critic and poet. Like Paraskos, Read used the fragmentary, subjective qualities of the journal form, but bent them towards a teleological arc in which the randomness of childhood experience became the providential origin of his own later artistic identity. Read's text thus provides a precedent, serving as a creative etiology for his life's work, which in turn gives us licence to read the Paraskos diary as a romantic act of self-narration and the true inauguration of the Cyprus College of Art as a work of art.

Central to the narrative form of the Paraskos diary is the way it records, or even constructs, a series of encounters between key figures, above all Paraskos and Bell, and the people and places of Cyprus in 1968. These encounters often resemble set pieces or scenes. They are not clichés, but *mise en scène* in which particular relations can be revealed. In this respect the text recalls the 'relational aesthetics' theorised by Nicolas Bourriaud, in which the artwork is constituted not by objects but by social relations and the situations they generate.[133] The Paraskos diary is full of such scenarios. There are the evenings spent drinking at Xenou's shop, the abortive attempts to buy Bell a pair of shoes and the excursions to Nicosia and Kyrenia. Each episode is less about the events themselves than the social relations enacted within them. Sometimes convivial, sometimes antagonistic, these moments together form a matrixial narrative of interconnected encounters. What the diary presents, therefore, is not simply a record of daily life but a proto-relational artwork, staging a social

---

[133] Nicolas Bourriaud, *Relational Aesthetics* (Dijon: Les Presses du Réel, 2002), 14

constellation that prefigures the establishment of the art school as a place made of stone, brick and mortar.

This suggests that the Paraskos diary needs to be viewed, not as a straightforward daily record of actual events, even if it was in some sense written in that way, but as a retrospective shaping of disorderly fragments into a recognisable plot structure. What might seem accidental or chaotic is organised through the writing process into a narrative of destiny. If this is viewed as a creative act in itself, it is worth paralleling with Paraskos's primary art form, painting, which was undertaken in an organic, but never chaotic, way. As Paraskos painted, elements of an image might emerge, evolve and even disappear, but only within the overall framework of the developing painting. A painting is thus 'emplotted' over time without being wholly predetermined, and the diary appears to operate in a similar way. As the text develops, its seemingly disorderly fragments are gradually resolved into a definable structure, a codification that renders the otherwise chaotic past intelligible. This process transforms the apparent accidents of life into a narrative of inevitability, so that the audience with Makarios seems not contingent, but predestined.

The movement from fragments to providential arc situates the Paraskos diary within a wider tradition of artists and writers who have aestheticised the episodic elements of lived experience into narratives of providential destiny. Yet what makes the diary distinctive as a literary form in which to do this is not only its internal structure but also its external function. It is both a personal record and a social document in the sense that it is a political and artistic document. If the diary can be seen to transform the chaos of lived experience into what seems like the inevitability of artistic destiny, it also situates that destiny within a social schema, which for Paraskos was the turbulent politics of Cyprus in 1968, as well as within Paraskos's wider practice as a visual artist. Here the diary resembles the forms analysed by Paperno in which diary writing itself becomes a creative practice that simultaneously inscribes both self and history.

To grasp the full significance of the Paraskos diary in this light we need to consider not only its teleological narrative but its status as an artwork and a political act embedded in a particular historical moment, particularly in light of the location of Cyprus in western Asia, and the early post-colonial context in which Paraskos was writing.

Parallels are useful in this context. In *Writing the Self, Writing the Nation*, Alexandra Katz looked at diaries written by Palestinians in which there was a blurring of the boundary between the individual expression of the self and the shared experience of historical events.[134] Palestinian diarists frequently inscribed themselves into national history, not always by commentary on political events, but by describing personal experiences that tracked the impact of political events. Within the Palestinian context this might seem an obvious situation for diarists as they have had to negotiate the restrictions and indignities placed on them by the State of Israel on a daily basis, as well as the ongoing impact of the *Nakba* of 1948. The situation in Cyprus, while not as extreme, parallels this to some extent as a post-colonial experience in which a colonial legacy of civil war and

---

[134] Kimberly Katz, 'Writing the Self, Writing History in Palestine,' in Batsheva Ben-Amos and Dan Ben-Amos (eds.), *The Diary: The Epic of Everyday Life* (Bloomington: Indiana University Press, 2020) 247

ultimately Western-backed external military intervention has been evident. What Katz suggests is that these kinds of experience find expression in both direct and indirect ways, and this seems to tally well with Paraskos's diary. Paraskos's irritations with judgemental and socially-conservative neighbours, his children's antics and Martin Bell's drunken collapses are always set against a backdrop of wider political turbulence.

There was a precariousness to life in Cyprus in 1968, when inter-communal strife was still evident, and external pressures from both the military dictatorship in Greece to the west and the belligerent state of Turkey to the north were mounting. These would culminate in the coup d'état instigated by Greece in 1974, and consequent war with Turkey the same year, in which Cyprus would lose almost half its territory.

In the Paraskos diary these elements can be intimated by the presence of British officials, such as Roy Jenkins, then the UK government's Chancellor of the Exchequer, in the narrative, as well as the looming figure of Makarios as both priest and president. At times the references in the diary border on comedy:

> The front page of a local newspaper carried a photograph of Mr Roy Jenkins, the British Chancellor of the Exchequer, over a caption saying that he is holidaying in Kyrenia and that he is staying in the Dome Hotel. Martin suggested that we go and see him and ask him to cash a cheque for us. Perhaps we could hire a photographer to take photographs of him which we could flog to a British newspaper.[135]

But the crucial point is that they are there, so that while the diary does not deliver political analysis in the formal sense, it nevertheless documents Cyprus's cultural and political atmosphere from below, embedding the artist's voice within a moment of transition from Cyprus being a colonial culture to a post-colonial one.

In this we can perhaps recast Paperno's concept of diaries as 'contracts of sincerity', by seeing in the idea not simply as a pact with the reader as to the veracity of what is written, but a sense that the self is inseparable from the still forming nation. Paraskos

---

[135] Appendix A.

wanted an audience with Makarios in order to establish what he saw as an essential component of any nation, an art institute, but this was tied up with his self identity as an artist. Ultimately these two components may have been unavoidably incompatible, as the requirements of a state art organisation are significantly different to the kind of creative space Paraskos envisaged. Nonetheless, the sought-for audience with Makarios was not only the climax of a personal quest for Paraskos, but a moment in which an individual artist's fate was tied to the formation of Cypriot nationhood. As a result, to tell one story was to tell the other, and it is notable that in the euphoria of the early twenty-first century attempts to create a two-state solution to the Israel-Palestine conflict, when progress seemed to be being made, similar arts organisations emerged in Palestine, such as ArtSchool Palestine and the International Academy of Art Palestine in Ramallah. Notably, both initiatives were also artist-led.

As Katz suggests of Palestinian diarists, the self becomes legible only within the frame of political struggle. Consequently, the diary is less a retreat from history than a way in which to enter into it. A similar lesson can be drawn from Salam Mir's 2019 study *Colonialism, Postcolonialism, Globalization and Arab Culture.* According to Mir the colonial frameworks of the late nineteenth and early twentieth centuries have persisted in the Arab world, both politically and culturally. Western powers constructed borders, imposed mandates and left enduring tensions through processes such as the 1917 Balfour Declaration. Through writing there is the potential for cultural resistance to these imperialist narratives even when the political leaderships in western Asia seem to acquiesce to them.[136] In various interviews Paraskos consistently asserted that the Cyprus College of Art was a Cypriot art school, not a transplanted western conception of an educational institution, and as a result both it and the diary can be framed as a form of creative resistance, both to the hostility of a number of individuals mentioned in the diary, but also against Western colonial narratives of Cyprus. Through the diary and the art school, Paraskos can be seen to have asserted a

---

[136] Salam Mir, 'Colonialism, Postcolonialism, Globalization, and Arab Culture,' in *Arab Studies Quarterly* 41, no. 1 (Winter 2019) 33–56

Cypriot presence and claim of agency that political exigencies threatened to deny.

This resistance is in itself an assertion of a non-canonical approach to art and culture, but the danger with all non-canonical approaches is that they simply serve to maintain social and cultural marginalisation. The disconnect between what a state requires of an art institution and what creative people like artists might require is profound and this tension is evident throughout the Paraskos diary in the hostility shown towards Paraskos and Bell. While this might seem paradoxical as Paraskos sought to create a Cypriot art institution in post-colonial Cyprus, its reasoning becomes clear once we recognise that in the post-colonial states that emerged in places like Cyprus after British rule the newly-emergent ruling classes often fully internalised a Western colonial conception of art and culture. Again we can see a parallel for this in the Arab world geographically adjacent to Cyprus. In *Art Without History?* Nada Shabout argues that Arab art has often been excluded from the category of 'art proper' even within the Arab world, relegated instead to the status of ethnography, material culture or derivative modernism.[137] This final category is perhaps most useful, when we think of Cyprus. Cyprus's identity is partially western, but its colonial experience and geographic position often placed it in a similarly marginalised category to non-western cultures within art historical narratives. I am old enough to remember going into the Witt Library at the Courtauld Institute of Art in London in the late 1980s, to examine the photographic archive, and finding Cypriot art catalogued under the heading 'Non-Asiatic Orientals'.[138] Certainly in 1968 Cyprus was geographically peripheral to Europe, politically unstable and culturally overlooked. In this context, the resistance offered by the Paraskos diary can be seen as an effort to insert a highly individualised version of Cypriot art into history on its own terms, rather than through the condescending gaze of the West and Westernised leaders in Cyprus. The very act of writing

---

[137] Nada Shabout, "Art Without History? Evaluating 'Arab' Art: An Introduction," in *Middle East Studies Association Bulletin* 42, no. 1/2 (Summer/Winter 2008): 16

[138] For parallel non-anecdotal comment, see Elena Stylianou and Nicos Philippou, 'Greek-Cypriot Locality: (Re) Defining our Understanding of European Modernity' in Pam Meecham, ed., *A Companion to Modern Art* (Hoboken: Wiley-Blackwell, 2018) 338–341

and archiving these episodes, even if they appear trivial and chaotic, becomes a way to assert that Cypriot cultural life belongs in and of itself the historical record.

If there is a problem at a macro level in asserting Cyprus into wider art histories, there there is also a problem at a micro level in gaining acceptance within Cyprus. The hostility of several locals to Paraskos and Bell, and the difficulty in gaining an audience with Makarios occur within the diary, but the marginalisation continues long afterwards. For Homi Bhabha, writing in *The Location of Culture*, colonial power survives not only through direct domination but through the way its cultural values are internalised by the colonised, producing forms of 'mimicry', an almost-but-not-quite repetition of Western models.[139] In Cyprus, the persistence of Western cultural hierarchies after independence means that legitimacy in the arts has often been measured against Western standards, with institutions accepted only if they resemble respectable-looking academies in the West, and with

---

[139] Homi K. Bhabha, *The Location of Culture* (London: Routledge, 1994) 85–92

artists only validated when recognised by what are deemed appropriate art institutions abroad.

This framework rendered Paraskos's project suspect. The diary records neighbours denigrating him and Martin Bell as 'beatniks', a label that signals not only local conservatism but also an internalised Western disdain for avant-garde forms. The Cyprus College of Art, when it emerged from these encounters, was artist-led, experimental and deliberately marginal to bureaucratic structures, a model that diverged from the state-approved institutional framework inherited from colonial administration. From the perspective of local officials and later gatekeepers of culture in steel-and-glass universities on the island, such a school appeared illegitimate precisely because it did not mimic the Western academy closely enough. Ironically, their very criteria for judgment, seriousness, propriety, institutional formality, were imported values used to justify colonialism in the first place, but now internalised to the point of becoming unquestioned markers of legitimacy.

This phenomenon of internalised judgement and marginalisation is not merely a historical anecdote from 1968. It continues to shape the academic and critical reception of Cypriot art today, as evidenced by *Contemporary Art from Cyprus Politics, Identities, and Cultures across Borders,* edited by Gabriel Koureas, Elena Stylianou and Evanthia Tselika.[140] This text is important both for being the first extensive exploration of contemporary Cypriot art and for having global reach through its publisher, the British publishing house Bloomsbury. This makes it possible to characterise *Contemporary Art from Cyprus* as being the representative of contemporary Cypriot art to the world, in a way local publications, including those of government agencies, are not.

Yet, *Contemporary Art from Cyprus* does not claim to be a comprehensive overview of contemporary Cypriot art, and in its self-declared partiality there is a tendency to prioritise neo-conceptualist practices, or what one of the editors and authors describes as 'socially engaged art practices'.[141] Although this seems

---

[140] Elena Stylianou et al (eds.), *Contemporary Art from Cyprus: Politics, Identities and Cultures across Borders* (London: Bloomsbury, 2023)

[141] Evanthia Tselika, 'Art, Conflict, and Antagonism,' in Elena Stylianou et al (eds.), *Contemporary Art from Cyprus: Politics, Identities, and Cultures across Borders* (London: Bloomsbury, 2022) 228.

to indicate the editors and authors wanted to frame the contemporary element in *Contemporary Art from Cyprus* in terms of ephemeral practices, such as art as a form of social engagement, temporary direct interventions and archival recording, this is not universally applied in the book, which also contains an extensive discussion of how Cypriot state and cultural institutions have canonised Christoforos Savva as the 'founding father' of modern Cypriot art, while marginalising what is seen as the equally significant contribution of Glyn Hughes.[142]

Inevitably the inclusion of Savva and Hughes sits uneasily alongside the more activist chapters, but it also raises the question as to why Paraskos was therefore excluded. I suspect there is no easy answer to this question, but for my part, I would argue that it stems from a fundamental misunderstanding of Paraskos's project, beginning with the diary. By taking the 1968 diary not as a record of fact, but as the first creative act in an almost six-decades long work of installation and

---

[142] Yannis Toumazis, 'Christoforos Savva and Glyn Hughes: The Untold Story of a Forgotten Partnership,' in Elena Stylianou et al (eds.), *Contemporary Art from Cyprus: Politics, Identities, and Cultures across Borders* (London: Bloomsbury, 2022) 121

performance art that included the Cyprus College of Art and the Great Wall of Lempa, we see Paraskos was not engaged in creating statements of monumental modernism that might have justified exclusion from the book (had its self-defined criteria been consistently applied), but in an extraordinarily long-lived form of socially-engaged, durational practice.

The Great Wall of Lempa, added to over decades by successive groups of students, artists and visitors, was never intended to be a finished monument but an evolving process of free association and mutual aid. Likewise, the Cyprus College of Art operated not as a top-down institution, but as a kind of anarchist autonomous zone, a space of collective labour, dialogue and differentiation, where individuality and community continually reshaped one another. In this, Paraskos's project had more in common with the socially engaged, participatory and ephemeral practices prioritised in *Contemporary Art from Cyprus*.

With this we return to the relationship of Paraskos and art establishment of Cyprus. Arguably there is a desire in that establishment to mimic the forms of art institution seen in the West, in what

Bhabha would call 'ambivalent mimicry'. This suggests Cypriot society after independence was neither fully autonomous nor simply colonised, but caught in a third space where Western criteria remained the measure of value as though that criteria had universal validity. Paraskos's insistence that the Cyprus College of Art was a Cypriot art space, not a branch of the global Western art world, directly challenged this false cultural consciousness, even as it gave space to an often glittering array of international artists. As a consequence, his diary does more than narrate a personal struggle, it exposes the ways in which Western cultural authority was sustained from within Cyprus itself long after independence, and on to the present day in academic texts, exhibition policies and the treatment of the Cyprus College of Art by the Government of Cyprus after the death of Paraskos in 2014.

    Paraskos's diary is far more than a simple record of events. Through its literary construction and performative sincerity, it functions as the inaugural act of his most significant work of art, the Cyprus College of Art. As a document of post-colonial assertion, it struggles against internalised marginalisation, using the intimate form of the diary to inscribe a defiantly Cypriot artistic identity into history. It is in the humble, spiral-bound pages of this text that the personal, the artistic and the political are irrevocably fused.

Chapter 6:
I Want to Break Free:
the folkloric trap

One of the most persistent features of the critical discussion surrounding Stass Paraskos is the recurrence of labels such as *naïve* in relation to his art. In early British criticism of Paraskos he was described by W. E. Johnson in 1970 as 'patently self-taught and naïve,' casting him as a Rousseau-like primitive whose art derived what little value Johnson believed it possessed from raw authenticity rather than skill or intellect.[143] In 2016, Derek Horton deployed similar language when he referred to Paraskos's paintings as having a 'naïve charm,' though here the term was wielded with evident condescension to imply that the work was slight, even insubstantial.[144] Even in the hands of a largely sympathetic critic, such as Merete Bates writing in *The*

---

[143] W.E. Johnson, 'A Second Look at Paraskos' in *The Northern Echo*, 22 May 1970, 7

[144] Derek Horton, 'Jonathan Trayte: Polyculture / Stass Paraskos: Lovers and Romances,' in *Corridor8* (review, 22 August 2016), online at https://corridor8.co.uk/article/review-jonathan-trayte-polyculture-stass-paraskos-lovers-and-romances-the-tetley-leeds/

Guardian newspaper in 1966, this narrative was used with Bates describing Paraskos as a 'peasant painter'.[145]

Whether apparently affirmative, as in Bates's romanticisation of Paraskos, or openly dismissive, as in Johnson and Horton, the implications are consistent. Paraskos is presented as an unschooled oddity, trapped within a framework that reduces his work to an exotic curiosity.[146] This interpretive pattern, which we might term the folkloric trap, has proven remarkably persistent in shaping how his art has been received. Indeed, so persistent is it that it has even entered the discourse of Cypriot art as written by Cypriots, with Eleni Nikita writing:

> In order to concentrate on the essential and archetypal, Stass Paraskos (1933-2014) consciously adopted an unsophisticated and naïve artistic vocabulary with expressionist and fauvist forms and depicted in representational

---

[145] Merete Bates 'Stass Paraskos' in *The Guardian*, 22 May 1970, 8
[146] See Panikos Panayi and Varnava Andrekos, 'Family, Migration and Murder in the Greek Cypriot Community in London' in *Historical Research* 95, no. 267 (2022) 84-87

language subjects from history and the life of his country.[147]

At best Paraskos is presented as a kind of ur-artist, channelling some essential and archetypal Cypriotness. But to occupy this position he must remain 'unsophisticated' and 'naïve', terms that imply the absence of intellectual agency.

This is the kind of critical bind Rasheed Araeen has identified, in which artists outside the white Western world have been denied recognition and consigned instead to the role of ethnic outsiders. A practising artist himself, Araeen's understanding of this issue arose from his personal struggles to gain acceptance in the London art world of the 1970s and 80s, a process that led him to found the journal *Third Text* in 1987.[148] This was a significant development as it provided a platform for those excluded to both highlight their own aims and, crucially, challenge the discourses imposed on them.

---

[147] Eleni Nikita, 'The Visual Arts: An Overview' in Miltos Miltiadou et al. (eds.), *Window on Cyprus* (Nicosia: Press and Information Office, 2015) 229
[148] Rasheed Araeen, *Art and Institutional Racism* (London: Austin Macauley, 2024) 93f

According to Araeen artists from outside the Western centres of modernism have been systematically excluded from the canon by being denied assimilation into the artistic systems typically adopted by the Western avant-garde. In essays such as 'Our Bauhaus, Others' Mudhouse'[149] and his framing of *The Other Story*, an exhibition he guest-curated for the Hayward Gallery in London in 1989, Araeen insisted that while Western artists were typically assessed in terms of form, innovation and conceptual rigour, artists from Asia, Africa, the Caribbean or the Mediterranean periphery were reduced to cultural representatives, valued for their ethnic qualities rather than their contribution to modern and contemporary art. As a result we can see the category of the ethnic artist functions as a trap, denying those placed in it all hope of being taken seriously as contemporary artists by insisting there is an inherent difference in their work or its underpinning from Western art. This is an insistence that is rooted in clichés of it being folkloric or decorative.

---

[149] Rasheed Araeen, 'Our Bauhaus, Others' Mudhouse,' in *Third Text* 1, no. 3 (1987) 3

This understanding of the position of non-Western artists in the Western art world finds an echo in the writings of another artist, Bedri Baykam. In his book *The Monkey's Right to Paint* Baykam set out the double standards by which Western and non-Western artists are judged, arguing that when a Western artist makes use of local or folkloric motifs it is hailed as an act of sophisticated postmodern play, whereas when a non-Western artist does the same it is read reductively as ethnographic or decorative.[150] The intercommunal parallel is notable here. Although Baykam came from Turkey and Paraskos from the Greek community of Cyprus, in the face of Western art criticism both were subject to the same structural relegation, with Orientalist frameworks flattening historical differences into a shared condition of marginality.

Baykam's deliberately provocative tone has drawn censure in academic circles,[151] perhaps underscoring his argument that institutional rejection is the predictable result for non-Western artists who

---

[150] Bedri Baykam, *Monkey's Right to Paint* (Istanbul: Literatür Yayıncılık, 1994)
[151] For example, Nadine Kibanda, *Review of Monkey's Right to Paint* in *Nka Review of Contemporary African Art* 11(2000) 116

challenge the dominant critical framework, a framework that also privileges the dispassionate academic voice over the polemical artistic assertion. But still his argument aligns with a broader postcolonial critique that emerged in the late twentieth century. Indeed, his polemical style of writing aligns more fully with that of Paraskos, and he articulates what scholars like Partha Mitter would later term the 'double bind' of the non-Western artist, effectively damned if they ignore their cultural heritage, and damned if they engage with it.[152] Non-engagement appears to lead to preclusion from the Western art discourse, while engagement is almost invariably interpreted through the reductive, ethnographic lens of the folkloric trap.

At a more academic level, Araeen, Baykam and Paraskos's understanding of their experiences as marginalised artists tallies well with the theories of Edward Said's analysis of Western Orientalism. In *Orientalism,* Said described how the West habitually constructed the 'Orient' as decorative, exotic, sensual and irrational, a foil against which Western rationality

---

[152] Partha Mitter, 'Decentering Modernism: Art History and Avant-Garde Art from the Periphery', in *The Art Bulletin,* vol. 90, no. 4 (December 2008) 537

and seriousness could be defined.[153] This logic applies as much to art criticism as to literature or politics.

For Said, Orientalism was not simply a question of misrepresentation, it was a process of reductivism or essentialisation. In all of the examples of critics cited, including that of the Cypriot writer Nikita, there is a desire to find 'essential and archetypal' Cypriotness in Paraskos's work. Undoubtedly, as a Greek-Cypriot Paraskos did embody a kind of Cypriotness, or even Cypriot Hellenicity, but the search for archetypal Cypriotness leads each writer on Paraskos to embrace clichés of Cypriot identity, rather than the reality of the artist's individual intellect or engagement with modernism and modernity. This desire for a stable, pre-modern Cypriot essence traps Paraskos in a discourse that either labels him in a reductive and inaccurate way, or excludes him from Western art discourses, or both. By framing Paraskos as naïve or a peasant he is placed firmly within a folkloric structure, so that even if his admirers and detractors treat his art as charming, it is always also unserious, decorative and unintellectual. To praise him for naïve

---

[153] Edward W. Said, *Orientalism* (New York: Pantheon Books, 1978) 72

charm or for embodying an archetypal Cypriotness is, in effect, to reproduce the Orientalist manoeuvre of aestheticising the other while denying him conceptual agency.

A direct expression of this Orienalist approach to Paraskos was apparent in 2006 when Paraskos challenged the attitude of the Manifesta organisation as it sought, unsuccessfully, to mount its peripatetic biennial of art in Cyprus under the banner, Manifesta 6. This can be read, through the lens articulated by Araeen, as an example of how Western art institutions carry within them inherited Eurocentric attitudes that may appear neo-colonialist or even racist to those on the receiving end, even where such readings conflict with the organisers' stated intentions.[154]

The official announcement for Manifesta 6 declared that the biennial would establish the island's first experimental art school and framed Cyprus as a peripheral location, not in Europe, although positioned in a peripheral zone at the newly expanded European Union's geographical limits. This would be a stage for

---

[154] See Rasheed Araeen, *Art and Institutional Racism* (London: Austin Macauley, 2024) especially 25f and 51f

re-thinking Europe's relation to the Middle East and North Africa.[155] The implication of this was unmistakable. Cyprus appeared as an empty or contingent cultural ground whose value lay in proximity and symbolism, not in its own institutions and histories.

Subsequent literature reinforced that idea. In *Notes for an Art School*, General Coordinator for Manifesta 6, Yiannis Toumazis explicitly attributed the shape of contemporary Cypriot art as deriving from 'the absence of a top-tier art school' on the island, casting the proposed Manifesta-led art school as the catalytic nucleus of something Cyprus lacked and needed. The island was described as 'remote and relatively unknown,' yet promising as a geo-cultural hub once the correct educational infrastructure was set in place. The use of this language institutionalised a narrative of absence, lack and need, presenting the biennial in a dominant role as benefactor and Cyprus's subservient position as recipient.

One of the key problems for Manifesta 6 in pursuing this intellectual line was Paraskos. A well-known Cypriot artist by this time, he was well aware

---

[155] **Manifesta 6 Press Release no. 1, 14 Feb 2005**

that Cyprus did have a top-tier art school, the Cyprus College of Art, as he had founded it in 1969. Ironically, it is also possible to argue that it had been developing since that time precisely along the lines espoused by Manifesta 6 in its publicity material. The Cyprus College of Art was an experimental, non-institutional, international art school, albeit one rooted in the local situation, rather than being sent from abroad.

When Paraskos complained publicly of this marginalisation of his long-running project, the response of the Manifesta 6 organisers evidently made matters worse. A hastily arranged site visit to the premises of the Cyprus College of Art in Lempa led to relations between Paraskos and Manifesta 6 worsening, as recounted by Paraskos in an article published at the time, entitled 'When Manifesta Came to Lempa.' According to Paraskos his Manifesta guests viewed the College and its iconic sculpture wall in silence. They were self-consciously indifferent to the handmade studios, built by visiting artists at the Cyprus College of Art over the decades and seemed to make a point of ignoring the group of international postgraduate students then working in those studios. Paraskos read this as barely disguised disdain, noting that, 'My Manifesta guests had nothing to say about it, not even a friendly remark as demanded by good manners.' Finally losing his own manners, Paraskos asked one of the visitors if Manifesta was a capitalist plot designed to take over Cypriot art.[156]

Clearly the experience confirmed for Paraskos that Manifesta's discourse was incapable of stepping outside its own Western neo-colonialist script, predisposed as it was to identify particular signifiers for contemporary art, and blind to manifestations of art that fell outside of it.

This was by no means an experience unique to Paraskos. In an *Open Letter to Manifesta*, written in January 2005, the highly-regarded Cypriot artist Helene Black objected to the use of the tragedy of Cyprus for artistic self-promotion. Honing in on Manifesta using imagery of the Green Line dividing Cyprus, accompanied by the jaunty tagline, *Wishing you all the best for 2005*, she suggested the group was trying to transform the Green Line from a political wound into a

---

[156] Stass Paraskos, 'When Manifesta Came to Lempa' in *ArtCyprus*, no. 2, Autumn 2026, 1

'cultural commodity' tradable on Western art markets. Like Paraskos, Black too suggested Manifesta resembled a subtle form of cultural colonisation.[157]

The paradox of this situation is eminently clear. Although Cyprus should not have been considered an artistic wasteland in need of a dose of Western artistic culture, let alone a *tabula rasa* ripe for colonisation by an external cultural force, it could have benefitted from the extraordinary power an organisation like Manifesta was able to muster in terms of financial resources and publicity. There is a sense of hurt in Paraskos's reaction to the snub by Manifesta, suggesting he recognised that much of its rhetoric could have been applied to his own Cyprus College of Art. Had the organisers of Manifesta been willing to build on existing structures like the Cyprus College of Art, the event could have put down deep roots in Cyprus, while also engaging in the globalised art world of the new millennium.

That Manifesta was incapable of doing this is shown, however, by Florian Waldvogel in his text *Notes for an Art School*, in which he doubled down on the

---

[157] 'Open Letter to Manifesta,' in NEME – New Media Museum, blog, last modified 15 May 2006, https://www.neme.org/blog/open-letter-to-manifesta.

paradox. Casting the proposed Manifesta 6 art school as uniquely distinctive because of its form as an 'exhibition or project… devoid of the general misery of the institutions,' Waldvogel called for transdisciplinary seminars, workshops, radio and library infrastructures that would 'overcome the separation of theory and practice'.[158]

Manifesta 6 can be seen as offering a paradigmatic example of the folkloric trap transposed into institutional form. Cyprus was cast as peripheral and empty, waiting for innovation, while Paraskos, whose prior work in Cyprus embodied many of the qualities Manifesta claimed to want, was erased from the narrative. It is arguable that this was not simply an act of oversight, but a repetition of an Orientalising discourse that could not acknowledge conceptual agency at the periphery.

When the Manifesta project collapsed in June 2006, the organisers and their supporters framed the debacle as resulting from local political intransigence, rather than the idea Manifesta 6 had a flawed philosophical underpinning at its heart. Only a small

---

[158] *Notes for an Art School: Manifesta 6* (Nicosia: Nicosia for Art, 2006) 20

number of writers have attempted a more nuanced critique of what went wrong. One, Andrea Liu, established a structural critique of the category of art biennial to which Manifesta belonged. Although they might seek to present themselves as counter-hegemonic correctives to global homogeneity, Liu suggested biennials still remained tethered to neoliberal circuits and a rhetoric of centre versus periphery. From this point of view, Manifesta 6 can be seen as having attempted to subordinate the global to the local through a narrative framework that represented Cyprus as lacking infrastructure and as a void to be filled by a 'bicommunal' school, that would in effect erase that which was local.[159] Consequently, what was presented as an anti-homogenising project, was seen on the ground, in the eyes of artists like Paraskos and Black, as an Orientalising pedagogy in which the periphery provided the problem only so the centre could supply the solution.

---

[159] Andrea Liu, 'Theorizing Art Interventions: Manifesta 6 and Occupy 38,' in Raqs Media Collective and Shveta Sarda (eds.) *Sarai Reader 9: Projections* (Delhi: Centre for the Study of Developing Societies, 2013)

In many ways the Manifesta 6 fiasco should probably be regarded as a footnote in the history of Paraskos, albeit one that illustrates well the dangers of the folkloric trap and the consequent marginalisation of artists like him by those who pursue a mainstream Western conception of art. More interesting are the attempts to recognise the positive qualities in the work of Paraskos in ways that manage, paradoxically, to maintain the binary system that is the folkloric trap.

A number of critics have sought to frame Paraskos as a hybrid figure, able to combine the folkloric elements of peripheral Cyprus with the modernist and contemporary elements of mainstream Western art. He is, in effect, commended for bringing these together in some kind of hybrid form. Yet, the interesting thing about Paraskos is not his capacity to combine these two seemingly contradictory frameworks, but that he exposes the artificiality of the categories themselves. It is a hybridisation that always seems to involve grafting the supplicant local or so-called peripheral onto the mainstream Western stock, and in that it is always going to give the Western discourse priority. Consequently, rather than seeing

Paraskos as hybrid, it might be more fruitful to see him for what he was, a disruptive figure whose life experiences, polemical writings and visual art practice exposed the artificiality of the oppositions through which his art is often read. Effectively, he stands closer to Araeen than we might at first imagine. Araeen's critique of the 'ethnic artist' label, and his insistence in both his writing and curatorial practice that non-Western artists be recognised as contributors to the formalist and conceptualist avant-gardes, sets out a template for thinking beyond hybridity. Araeen has not been content to be positioned as the bearer of cultural difference, rather he sought to show that his practice destabilised the very discourses of form and concept that underpins Western modern and contemporary art.[160]

    Paraskos, albeit in a different register, operated similarly. By collapsing categories such as school/artwork, monument/environment, or centre/periphery, he revealed the contingency of the Western art-historical binaries in which he was being contained.

---

[160] Rasheed Araeen, 'A New Beginning: Beyond Postcolonial Cultural Theory and Identity Politics,' in *Third Text* 14, no. 50 (Spring 2000) 5

More recently, artists such as Hew Locke have enacted comparable disruptions. Locke's sculptural assemblages make use of colonial iconography and decorative excess in ways that simultaneously embrace and destabilise the categories of folk, craft, ornament and political art. Like Paraskos, Locke is sometimes praised as a hybridiser of tradition and contemporary art, but his work too can more usefully be read as a critique of the structures that render *tradition* and *contemporary* legible in the first place. Araeen, Locke and Paraskos exemplify how artists from the periphery do not merely supplement Western art with folkloric colour, they interrogate and destabilise the conceptual boundaries on which its hegemony rests.

If Eleni Nikita, in her description of Paraskos as both 'unsophisticated and naïve' yet 'consciously' adopting such a stance, has already revealed a critical contradiction, she also illustrates a paradoxical structural dynamic that is inherently unstable. This paradox undermines itself in assertions such as Paraskos was *consciously* naïve. The consciously naïve cannot be naïve at all. But the gesture points to something more than critical imprecision. It exposes how Cypriot criticism itself has at times absorbed and reproduced the very categories imposed by the Western art world, re-inscribing the folkloric trap from within. To borrow Homi Bhabha's language of mimicry, local critics may echo the Western discourse almost exactly, yet not quite, so that Paraskos is celebrated for embodying 'essential Cypriotness' while simultaneously denied conceptual agency. What appears as affirmation, with the naming of him as archetypal, rooted and authentic, serves in practice to stabilise the binary between the peripheral and the metropolitan. As a result, the folkloric trap does not simply arrive from without, but is internalised and redeployed within Cypriot critical discourse, a pattern that helps explain why Paraskos has remained so consistently positioned as an ethnicised curiosity rather than a disruptive interlocutor of contemporary art.

In saying this I am aware that we risk making another fundamental error, that of reducing Paraskos to the role of passive object in the discourse of art in Cyprus. This again risks re-inscribing the binary divisions that his work unsettles. A more meaningful reading is to recognise that, although Cypriot criticism has often re-imposed the Western folkloric trap, Paraskos sought to dismantle it from within, not as the victim of an Orientalising discourse, but as a disruptive agent who rendered the neat oppositions of naïve/contemporary, centre/periphery and folkloric/conceptual unstable and porous. His repeated insistence that he was not a naïve artist stands as an explicit counter to Nikita's claim that he was.

In this, Paraskos's position parallels a broader set of non-Western strategies that have sought not simply to bridge, but to fracture, the binaries imposed by Western art criticism. Araeen's practice and writings, for instance, represent a strategy of refusal, a determined rejection of the 'ethnic artist' label and a demand for parity of critical language. Araeen insisted that his geometric, constructivist-oriented works be read within the same formalist and conceptual frameworks applied to Western minimalism, refusing the ethnographic lens through which his art was routinely viewed. By contrast, Hew Locke's approach has been one of strategic play. Rather than refusing hybridity, he performs and exaggerates it, deploying decorative excess and colonial ornament to expose the power structures underpinning Western art history and museology. What we can see here is that Paraskos occupied a position between these two modes. Like Araeen, he resisted being cast as ethnic or naïve, yet, like Locke, he turned the materials and symbols of his culture, its mythic narratives, folkloric motifs and vernacular forms, into vehicles for critique. His art does not merely synthesise the modern and the folkloric, it reveals the instability of those categories, showing that the lines separating centre from periphery, intellect from instinct, and the modern from the traditional, are themselves fictions imposed by the Western canon in order to maintain the Western canon. From this position we can argue Paraskos participated in a wider de-colonial gesture, rejecting the inclusion of the periphery into the centre, by undoing the very distinction that makes such inclusion seem necessary.

What emerges from this sequence of critical framings and counter-framings is not simply a local misunderstanding of Paraskos, but a symptom of a broader epistemological structure, what Said meant when he identified Western Orientalism, and what might, in the Cypriot context, be more precisely described as its folkloric trap. That trap operates by aestheticising difference, transforming cultural specificity into charm and presenting it as naturalised and normal, in order to disarm its intellectual and political charge. To step outside this system, as Paraskos did, is not to reject the local but to refuse its weaponisation as a sign of otherness. His work anticipated a broader de-colonial turn in artistic practice, one that has neither sought assimilation within Western narratives of modernism nor indulged in a retreat into essentialised identity. Instead it has exposed the instability of both.

Like Araeen, Paraskos insisted on the right to be read as a thinker, and like Locke, he reclaimed the decorative as a site of critique. But in doing so, from the particular location of Cyprus, at once European and non-European, colonial and postcolonial, centre and periphery, he rendered visible the cracks in the entire edifice of Western art history and practice. The result is never a hybrid synthesis, but a sustained act of disruption, an art that refused to resolve the contradictions that produced it, and in doing so, revealed those contradictions as the very ground on which meaning could be made.

Appendix A

Stass Paraskos's Diary from the summer of 1968

20th July 1968: In Larnaca, Cyprus. Mary, the children and myself went to explore the town. I wanted to see what had changed. St Lazarus Square has changed a lot since old days. The long lean columns and colonnade has gone and the giant gate to the south of the church has been demolished. An ornate plaque tells us this modernisation has been carried out at the expense of one of the hotels on the square, which just happens to give residents at the hotel an uninterrupted view of St LazarusChurch.

We headed to the beach where Margaret and I went for a walk and found sixpence in the sand. I used it to buy Margaret an ice cream. Martin and Christine joined us at the beach. Martin was wearing a shirt and his swimming trunks but no trousers. He sat on a stone for five minutes, then took his shirt off and walked two or three yards into the shallow sea to a point where the water covered his feet well below the knee. He sat down, wet his trunks, got up, and then very slowly walked out again. He put his shirt on, lit a cigarette, sat on the same stone for a few minutes more and went home again. Martin had been for a swim.

21st July 1968: I woke up very early and sat listening to a music programme on the radio. An unstamped envelope addressed to "Mr Paraskos Ici" was thrown in under the floor. No doubt an abusing letter I thought.

It was only a note from Martin which ran like this:

"Dear Stass (my business partner).

A list of things I need:

1. Typewriter for a day or an evening.
2. Anthology of modern Cypriot poetry, to translate.
3. The Archbishop.
4. Rimbaud's mountain.
5. Paphos.

Other things possibly later. We must get this book right (a) to produce a good book; (b) to possibly produce a best seller to make our fortunes. I sharpen my pencil, half way."

22nd July 1968: Martin and myself went to Nicosia early to hang my exhibition. The pictures were already hung so we spent the time drinking in different places. We even had two very expensive beers in the Hilton.

By 5pm Martin was very drunk. I wasn't so bad because I did not drink as much and also because of a neurotic anxiety I get every time I have a new exhibition.

We went back to the gallery to wait for the guests and the Minister of Education, who was to open the show with a short speech.

On the right hand side wall as you go through the main entrance to the Hilton Hotel is an instrument which looks like a telephone except that instead of the receiver it has a hand microphone attached to it. I pointed it out to Martin who immediately picked it up and announced, 'I am here!'

Seconds later a uniformed bellboy came running towards us. Martin said he wanted to see the manager. When the manager arrived Martin said that we had spent the whole day preparing a good exhibition for the benefit of the hotel and its customers. Now it was the turn of the manager to do something for us. Martin put forward three demands on behalf of both of us: first that the manager shows us where to have a bath; second that he sees that our shoes are shined; and third that we have two free drinks. Each.

The manager gave us a professional smile, showed us where to have a shower, promised to see to the rest of our needs and disappeared. Next time we saw him was three days later when we went to check if we had sold any paintings. We did not remind him of his broken promise as concerned the shoeshine and free drinks.

Martin went for a shower and I for a three shilling coffee (tip included). When we met again we discovered that Martin had lost his last six shillings. We both went to the showers looking for it, but some bloody millionaire staying in the hotel must have found it first.

26th July 1968: In the evening Martin and me were drinking beer outside Xenou's. After a few pints Martin announced that he was taking Christine to town for a week, excused himself and went to collect her from their house across the road. A few minutes later I saw them walk together towards the town. 30 to 40 yards away Martin lost his balance and then went from one side of the road to the other hitting walls and hedges. When he went to collect Christine he must has swallowed a bottle of brandy in a matter of minutes. Both Martin and Christine hide bottles of brandy in the house. I think this is done to protect each other from excessive drinking, but in reality it just means there is a lot of alcohol around for them both to drink.

1st August 1968: One the plans before we came to Cyprus was that Martin and me would live in a monastery for a week. It was time to pay a visit to one of these monasteries to see what they are like. We chose Stavrovouni, which is visible from our street and is only 25 miles north-west of Larnaca on top of a 2000 foot mountain. We hired a taxi that drove us up the primitive and dangerous road. On arrival we were greeted by a notice at the entrance which informed us in Greek and English that entry to the monastery was strictly prohibited to people not decently dressed. "No lipstick, no short sleeves and no short trousers" the sign read. The monk in charge offered to lend Martin and Christine long sleeved shirts but we carried jackets and jumpers in the boot of the car and put these on. Despite the heat Mary put her overcoat on. Martin spent all his time up there feeding about fifteen cats with cheese, much to the disgust of two peasant women. Later at lunch Martin disappeared to the toilets. He was gone a long time and after a while Christine went to find him. When she returned she said Martin had lost his tool in his trousers and couldn't urinate.

3rd August 1968: I went to collect the pictures from the Hilton for my next exhibition in Larnaca. I could only carry about half of them in the taxi. I was told that one of the paintings was bought by the Ministry of Education for the Presidential Palace but I did not know which one. A few days later I went to Nicosia again to fetch the rest of my paintings. A message said that if I take the painting bought for the President to the Palace I will get paid. My inquiries to find out which one it was proved that I had already taken it to Larnaca a few days before. I promised to bring it back when the exhibition in Larnaca was over.

My exhibition in Larnaca was opened in the Four Lanterns by Mr Demetriou, the Minister of Commerce and Industry, who comes from Larnaca. Very poor attendance - mostly children. The only fun I had out of the show was from a little scandal. Neither the Mayor nor the members of his City Council showed up as they should have done, this being the normal thing when a cabinet minister is performing a function.

Some people thought the Mayor was offended because he was not invited to open the exhibition himself. But I joked that I thought a more likely explanation was that I had sent the invitations to the wrong place. In the back of my mind I wondered if my joke was true, but later I was told these eminent local dignitaries refused to appear because I did not invite them personally.

Apparently the Mayor said: 'I found a little card on my desk. Do you call this an invitation?' Some people said he went fishing instead, and that the starting of his motorboat was timed to coincide with the Minister's speech.

I was standing next to the Minister while he was making his speech when Paulo came to join me and asked very loudly: 'What is he talking about?' As I wasn't paying attention to the Minister I could not tell him.

8th August 1968: Martin went for a swim and nearly drowned. He had to be carried ashore by two men.

12th August 1968: We all went to the cinema and saw *The Long Arm of the Law* which we enjoyed enormously. But all the way home we had been closely followed by six youths who were making remarks about Christine and Mary which spoiled our conversation and our enthusiasm for the funniest scenes from the film. We pretended not to notice them although my blood was boiling with anger. At some stage I heard Martin ask Christine in a whisper whether he should scare them off with his schoolmaster voice. This alarmed me because two of the youths were almost twice the size of Martin.

Apart from this we had the children with us and there was nobody else about at that midnight hour. However we continued our walk without incident until we came to our house. Martin's place is only about 100 yards away from mine but we are separated by a corner. When we branched off I thought all the thugs followed Martin and Christine, I rushed Mary and the children in and turned around to see if the rest of the company was all right. To my uncontrollable anger I saw one of the youths standing opposite my house under a street lamp. Automatically I picked up a large stone from the ground, shouted in Greek, 'Did you have a good look?' and threw it at him with all my might. I missed, but I made him run towards the others, with me right on his heels in hot pursuit, armed with two more of the stones which abound in our unpaved street. When I turned the corner I shouted to Martin, 'Catch the bastards,' at the same time discharging my load of stones and swearing violently. I saw Martin make a move but they were too fast for us and escaped towards the beach. Poor Christine, who did not realise what was happening, was terrified. When she saw them running she thought they were making an attack on her and Martin.

In the meantime the whole neighbourhood woke up and people came out in their pyjamas and underwear. Others were looking out of their windows.

After we were assured by the neighbours that thugs like that will not be allowed in the neighbourhood any more, we went to sleep. But in the confusion I failed to inform Christine of this assurance and next morning I heard that she sat up all night with the strong stick by her side waiting for an assault.

14th August 1968: Martin, myself, Stanley and Margaret went to town to send a telegram to Kevin Crossley-Holland of Macmillan's: 'Desperate money. Telegraph Arts Council grant.' Before we returned, we checked to see if any of my pictures had sold. We found the gallery was open but in darkness with all the curtains drawn and lights out. Gave up hope of any sale. Very depressed.

The front page of a local newspaper carried a photograph of Mr Roy Jenkins, the British Chancellor of the Exchequer, over a caption saying that he is holidaying in Kyrenia and that he is staying in the Dome Hotel. Martin suggested that we go and see him and ask him to cash a cheque for us.

Perhaps we could hire a photographer to take photographs of him which we could flog to a British newspaper. My idea was to send him an invitation to the exhibition. On this last idea, not requiring travel and expense, we acted immediately. I asked the hotel receptionist for paper and an envelope and wrote a short note to Mr Jenkins.

Mr Jenkins and myself are not complete strangers. He was the Home Secretary in 1966 when two of my paintings were seized from a Leeds exhibition by the police and I was accused and subsequently convicted of indecency under the Vagrancy Act.

After my conviction I wrote to the MP Tom Driberg giving him the facts of the case and he kindly took the matter up with the Home Office. A few days later he wrote saying, amongst other things, that: 'I feel sure that had the decision to prosecute or not to prosecute been within the discretion of the Home Secretary there would have been no prosecution.

The main positive thing which Mr Jenkins said was this: 'I am to let him know when you next have an exhibition of your paintings in London, and he will make a point of coming along to see them.' In my invitation note I reminded Mr Jenkins of this episode.

16th August 1968: 7am, visited by Martin. He had telegram from Kevin Crossley-Holland saying Arts Council is contacting him directly. I expressed the fear that this money will not arrive before we leave the island. But Martin disagreed and said that it will be here any day, probably that same day. He proceeded to tell me about his excellent economic prospects for the next few days and composed a number of telegrams he was despatching to different good friends in London who were going to rush to the rescue. This ritual happens every time he wants to borrow a pound.

We went to Xenou's grocery shop and made three telephone calls. First one to the bank: did they have any money for Mr Bell? The answer was no. Next call to the gallery. Did they sell any pictures? The answer was no. And the third call was to Hilton hotel in Nicosia: did they receive the money for the picture sold to the Ministry of Education? The answer, once more, was no.

Martin wondered aloud how much credit could one have at Xenou's and ordered a pint bottle of beer. He had no money at all and I was down to my last 30 shillings, although I tried to give him the impression I was completely broke. In our depression we drank the beer very quickly and Martin ordered several other bottles which stood open on our table. He said he feels insecure if he sees only one bottle in front of him. Then he confided in me that Christine did not have anything to eat for the previous 24 hours. He himself could take hunger, but Christine.... She is such a good girl and, apart from her teeth, very attractive too.

I could see tears clouding his eyes and I felt embarrassed. Tears from a grown man always make me feel uncomfortable. He went on to tell me that he met Christine on a visit to Edinburgh. She was already living with a man, but when Martin got back to London he sent her some poems just the same. He said the nasty boyfriend made her write a very rude letter to him which caused her to break their association.

Some time later there was a poetry festival at London's Albert Hall. He went there hoping to meet her and, miraculously, did meet her in the bar. After that they went off and stayed together. He asked if I knew how he had met his first wife. He said he went to the Duke of York, a pub off Charlotte Street in London, for a drink and met this girl who said she was pregnant. He liked her, so he told her, 'Okay, I'll look after you.'

Her baby was a girl and later she had another daughter, this time with Martin. They had an agreement between them that they should stay together until the children grew up. This made him work as a teacher for 20 years, hating every minute of it. His wife's ambition on the other hand was to become a teacher herself. The strange thing was that, in the year they separated, he gave up teaching while his wife had qualified and got a teaching job.

When he told his wife about Christine she said that it was a typical case of an old man falling in love with the young girl. He is 27 years older than Christine and 10 years older than his wife.

I lent Martin a pound and immediately he went home. A few minutes later he came back and finished his beer.

17th August 1968: Mary and myself went to Nicosia to take the President's painting hoping that we might meet him. At the Hilton Hotel, where we went first, we were presented to a Mr Pavlos who said he would take the picture to the presidential Palace himself. He also took with him a receipt he asked me to sign saying I had received the sum of £60. Half an hour later he returned and with a serious expression informed me that there had been a mistake. (I assumed the worse). The price of the sold picture in the exhibition catalogue, he said, was marked for £75 while on my receipt I put £60. Since the Archbishop had already authorised payment of £75 do I mind accepting that? I said that I did not mind at all and that the last thing I wanted to do was get anyone into trouble. He paid me, and Mary and I went to town for a double lunch each.

19th August 1968: We all went to the Troodhos mountains by taxi to see where Rimbaud worked when he was in Cyprus. We set off from Larnaca at 7:30am and arrived at about 12 noon, after two stops. Martin was drunk and slept part of the way in spite of the noise from the children.

15 miles from Larnaca we ran over a snake crawling across the main road.

On arrival we decided to look up Mr Pefkios Georgiades, an architect we met at my exhibition who is working for the Ministry of Education and is on holiday with his family up there. We had some difficulty finding his bungalow because there are quite a few of these government residences spread on several hills. They are lent to civil servants for their vacations.

Another difficulty was that we did not know our friend's rank and since protocol was observed in allocating these houses we did not know where to look for him. The higher ranks in the service stay nearer the summit, with Government House, which Rimbaud helped to build, standing high above them all for use by the President and senior ministers. Luckily we met our friend outside a shop which sold everything from toys to coffee and alcoholic drinks. He was pleased to see us and bought drinks all round. He also suggested we should stay a few days, so we paid our taxi driver and sent him back to Larnaca.

We went to our friend's place for lunch. The table was laid under a group of high pine trees and he barbecued meat for us on an open fire built outdoors. My son Paulo said he was not going to eat mucky meat cooked in that way and the other children made similar remarks. But the meat was delicious and the rest of us ate with great appetite. In fact, for a couple of hours, we ate everything our friend could produce as soon as it came from the fire. We also drank a lot of his excellent wine, except Martin who drank brandy and a very strong alcoholic drink made in Cyprus called zyvania. That was a mistake. Suddenly Martin decided he wanted to go home. He was offered a bed to rest for a couple of hours but insisted on going home to sleep in his own bed. Luckily Christine was able to get him inside and put him to bed where he fell asleep. Free from Martin the rest of us went exploring and we found a hotel called the Jubilee that gave residents the choice to sleep inside in its rooms, or outside under the trees in tents. We chose the tents.

Unfortunately the time we chose to visit our friend was not happy one for him. His wife, who was pregnant, had suffered a haemorrhage a few days earlier, and had only got out of bed on the day of our arrival. A little son of his, who suffers from a very serious illness, caught cold and was complaining of a pain on the left side of his waist. Our friend's elderly mother was also ill and kept going to bed for a little rest every half hour or so. Our arrival clearly did not make things easier for them. Our kids are noisy and very curious with other people's property. Coffee was spilt, cakes and biscuits eaten, and antique plates were broken.

When Christine informed everybody that the toilet was broken I felt ashamed and offered to try and fix it. 'I'm very good at this sort of job,' I said. Christine and the children followed me and we crowded the lavatory to capacity. It seems that that a link in the mechanism that controls the water supply to the toilet had broken off and disappeared down the drain. Of course I could not fix it and fearing more disaster I suggested we cut our losses and head for the hotel. Christine went to wake up Martin but he would not come out. He wanted another brandy and a cigarette. Christine came out to borrow my matches. In my mind's eye I imagined the little house going up in flames.

There was no fire, but Martin's demands increased and his language became stronger. He would only go to Leeds and to no other place he insisted. In the meantime three of the children had disappeared into the forest. I thought if I take a walk while waiting for Martin's decision as to whether he would get out of bed or not, I could look for the children. It was getting dark and Mary was worried.

Passing round of the side of the house I saw through a window our friend's wife struggling to mend the toilet. I moved on quickly. The children were not to be found anywhere. I shouted out their names and searched until I was exhausted, but no use. Mary and our hosts joined the search. Some time later Christine came out of the house, but she was raging with anger, swearing and cursing Martin. He humiliates her and makes her violent, she said, everywhere they go. She suggested that I go and shout at him to get out, or else we could just drag him out by his hands and feet. I declined both ideas and suggested instead that Christine join the search for the children. All the while Martin could be heard shouting for her and cursing.

The missing children were found half a mile down the hill playing by a stream. When we got back to the house it was 7pm and Martin was still in bed.

Christine was still eager for me to go into the bedroom and shout at Martin, and by now I was very annoyed at all that had happened and was ready to quarrel with him. I marched into the bedroom and said, 'Martin we've got to go now.' Without a word of protest Martin jumped up from the bed with the word, 'Right!'

On the veranda I apologised to our hosts for all the trouble we had caused and thanked them for their hospitality. As we were driven to our hotel I noticed Martin carrying a large bottle of brandy he had somehow acquired from the house. When the hotel management gave us the choice of staying indoors or out, we chose two tents outside, one for Martin and Christine and the other for Mary, myself and the children.

After dinner we all went straight to bed at 9pm, and I was hoping for a long sleep in those peaceful surroundings after the trying day. But it wasn't to be. Martin, having slept most of the day, drank his brandy and talked to himself or to Christine right through the night. This did not seem to stop any of the children sleeping as soon as they hit their beds, but it was impossible for me.

After some maddening sleepless hours, I left the tent and walked up a hilltop where the only sound I could hear was the lovely breathing of the pine trees. There I slept on the ground until dawn. I watched the moon go down and then the sun rise before I went back to the tent. I also made a decision — never to travel with Martin Bell again.

At noon we went to the centre of the small resort to get a taxi back home. Pefkios came to say goodbye and we learned that his wife was losing blood again. This made me take another decision — not to speak to Bell again.

21st August 1968: Early morning visit by Martin. He wanted me to ring up the bank to see if his money had arrived. He was so drunk that he could just about stand on his feet. Together we went around to Xenou's shop where the telephone is and rang up. There was no money. Martin ordered drinks and suggested that we go to town and send a telegram to Charles Osborne of the Arts Council to see what is happening. I agreed.

Anthony Vernis, an old school teacher of mine and a friend, came to join us. Conversation turned to the events in Czechoslovakia, which was invaded by the Russians. We decided to send a letter of protest to a newspaper. We composed several, some in Greek and some in English, and signed them. But we could not decide how to describe ourselves; were we Communists', 'ex-Communists', 'Marxists', 'moderates', 'liberals', or what? Martin declared

himself an ex-communist and a music critic, and signed
himself accordingly. Following his lead I declared myself an
anarchist and an artist and we ordered more drinks. We
stuffed the letters in our pockets ready to post, but they
remained there until the end of our stay and were never
sent.

Suddenly Martin remembered that a 'certain party'
was bullying him and so he wanted to borrow a pound to
take to her. I obliged and Martin disappeared with my money
for the rest of the day.

22nd August 1968: I went to the beach with the family.
An hour later Christine came to remind me of an
arrangement I had with Martin to go to town to see if the
money from the Arts Council had arrived. Martin also
needed some shoes, and to send telegrams to Charles
Osborne and Peter Porter. Martin was supposed to be
waiting for me on the steps of my house, but he was not
there so I went to his place and found him lying on his bed
stone drunk. He must have drunk a bottle of brandy in the
half hour between Christine leaving him and my arrival.

Christine made several attempts to get him up, but he
would not move. I saw her getting angry and went across to
Xenou's for a drink; I did not wish to witness the scene.
From there I could hear shouting and fighting.

When the bus came I shouted Christine to leave him alone and that I could do the job by myself. She came to the door and I saw that she was in tears.

Later I wrote a letter to Peter Porter for whom Martin has a special affection:

> Dear Peter.
>
> Our journey is beginning to turn into a nightmare. Martin has been drunk at all hours of every day we have been here and you can imagine what this has done to his health. He begins the day with brandy before sunrise, turns to beer, then onto ouzo and back to brandy again at night. The only break from drinking he has is during the few hours he sleeps. As for food, he doesn't touch it unless Christine forces him to.
>
> All this leads to fights – sometimes violent – between himself and Christine which is not doing any good to anybody's morale and dignity. He has weakened himself so much that even going to the local cinema by taxi makes him tired.
>
> Another complication that makes things worse is a serious shortage of money. All he received since we arrived was a small sum from Leeds University. I

have lent him about £100 which was meant for my fare back home, and so now I am broke myself and also stranded. For this reason I have written to my bank asking for new fares in spite of an agreement I have made with them that if I needed to borrow more I would leave immediately for England. Martin and Christine have paid for their return fares but they need extra cash to pay some bills they have run up. They also need spending money for the journey home, which takes six days. Do you think you can hurry the Arts Council to send the £200 they have promised him?

I hate to alarm you but I think that the sooner we leave Cyprus the better. Martin has promised to see a doctor about his alcoholism as soon as we return.

Regards to your family.

With all respect,
Stass Paraskos

23rd August 1968: My ex-teacher Anthony came to see me this morning and brought two judges from the law courts and their wives with him. One of them, Judge George Pikes, comes from my village and is the youngest judge Cyprus has ever seen. He is also a relative by marriage, having married my cousin last month. They left with two pictures, both bought by Judge George, who said he will send the money with Anthony. With the opportunity of this visit I also gave his wife a framed drawing as a wedding present.

Afterwards, Martin and I paid our daily visit to the bank to find out if his money had arrived. Martin was in his slippers because he had no shoes. There was no money at the bank and so we went to the Larnaca Taverna on the seafront and drank beer. Martin talked to me about 'The Group', a poetry society he had helped to start, but he confided to me that he had been very treacherous to the other members. After he got what he wanted (he did not specify what, but I understood that this was Christine) he dissolved in the group.

I was amused to hear Martin say this because all the other members of this group I have ever met seemed to me to be smarter, tougher and certainly more successful then he has ever been. Some are now well-known personalities in the world of criticism and journalism.

A group of young women passed by and I remarked that one of them looked like somebody we know. At this Martin turned down the edges of his mouth, showed his front teeth and after a pause said he would kill me if I slept with Christine. His mouth always takes this shape when he becomes emotional.

My son Stanley says Martin gets it from the cats that seem to be attracted to him when he sleeps and of which he is especially fond. I protested that I am not in the habit of sleeping with my friend's wives, no matter what the temptation.

This incident did not surprise me much because I know Martin to be very possessive where Christine is concerned. On several occasions when we have sat drinking on his verandah he has insisted on Christine going to bed with him when he was unable to continue, just so she would not stay up with me. At other times, when Christine was on the beach, and we sat outside Xenou's, he would interrupt his drinking every so often to go and see what she was doing. Once he even told me, with some malice, that Stanley, who is 11 years old, is in love with Christine.

On leaving the Larnaca Tavern Martin was too drunk to walk home and so we crossed the road to catch a taxi outside the hotel where I had my exhibition. As we passed by the wife of the owner saw me and called me to say that I had a letter. It was from Mrs Roy Jenkins thanking me for the invitation to her husband and regretting that they couldn't visit Larnaca to see my pictures because their stay in Cyprus was short and the drive to Larnaca too long.

As soon as we got back to my place Martin proceeded to finish off a bottle of ouzo he had left there before we went into town. I read two letters I found on the table. One was from my bank manager in England saying he was not in a position to meet my request for more money until my overdraft was paid off. The other letter was from

Eric White of the Arts Council. Every time this good man writes to me he gives some friendly words and cheerful information. This time he said that Martin's confirmation letter had been sent and all Martin had to do now was to write back to say he accepts the grant he has been offered. After that a cheque will follow.

I tried to make Martin write the letter of acceptance to send to the Arts Council but he said he was not in a writing mood. Instead he drank some more ouzo and fell asleep on the chair. Christine tried to wake him up but it was no good. We decided that I should write a letter and get him to sign it in the morning. With Christine writing and I dictating we began like this:

Dear Sir,

I am very grateful to the Arts Council…

At this Martin jumped up shouting that he is not grateful to anybody and swearing violently against us, the Arts Council and the ever-gentle Eric White. In this state he managed to find his way out of my place and disappeared up the street. A few moments later we heard him scream, like somebody being attacked. Christine ran out after him saying he has fallen down again.

In the evening Martin came to see me. From his fall he was badly cooked on the forehead, nose and around a blood-red left eye. His upper lip was also swollen and he looked in a terrible state. He wanted me to go round to Xenou's to buy him a bottle of ouzo because in the condition his face was in he did not dare go himself. I said I'll do it if we write the letter to the Arts Council. He answered that he would write the letter if I buy the ouzo first. We compromised: young Stanley would go for a bottle of beer which we'd drink while writing the letter together. As soon as he had finished writing the letter I promised I would go for the ouzo. And so it was done.

We posted the letter in the little yellow postbox round the corner and then all sat down to celebrate this event with ouzo and beer, drinking until well into the night as though it was a major achievement.

26th August 1968: Martin's face is terribly swollen. He refuses to see a doctor on the grounds that hispowers of recovery are enormous. We talked at length about three new cat friends he has made. This was a day of the cats. First thing in the morning the children and I found an abandoned kitten on the beach. Stanley put it in his inflatable rubber boat to try to get it around some rocks in the sea, but it managed to fall overboard. The little thing looked terrible and was shivering when we fished it out and got it safely to the beach. Word was sent to Christine and she came running with some bread for it to eat. Then she left only to return a few minutes later with a packet of butter. She sat on the sand, the kitten in her lap, dipping her finger into the butter and feeding the cat.

Later she was joined by Englishwoman in a bikini whom we had seen on the beach several times before. We knew her vaguely and called her the army wife because she was the wife of an English soldier serving at the British base. Eventually the army wife picked up the kitten and said she was going to take it home with her. As she passed by me she stopped and asked if I had been trying to drown it. I tried to explain the accident but it didn't sound convincing.

When she had gone Christine said the army wife had taken the cat because she had said we could not be trusted to look after it properly.

That evening we all had dinner in the yard of a small restaurant called the Garden of Allah but a more appropriate name would have been the garden of cats. Half a dozen of them sat begging at our feet during the meal. Martin also brought up the subject of his three new cat friends several times. 'Duckie, it breaks your heart to make friends with cats and then to have to leave them.' All evening Martin, Christine and the children had a great time playing with the restaurant cats, to the great annoyance of Mary who saw a health hazard in handling and feeding dirty animals with the same fingers one uses to eat.

Christine remarked about a large ginger tomcat sitting on the restaurant wall. Martin said there was no such thing as a ginger tomcat – all ginger cats are female he said.

Christine accused him of being dogmatic. In a small place like Cyprus, she said, where cats inbreed like mad, everything is possible. Martin pleaded that even if that is true she must not demolish a view he had held for over twenty years. The argument went on, Lasting until the end of a very long dinner.

27th August 1968: The house next to Xenou's is owned by a man named George. He has a long record of prison sentences for political crimes, like singing The Internationale, marching without permission and protesting outside government offices. Every night he sits outside Xenou's shop and tell stories of his adventures if there is an audience who will listen; if not he just sleeps on his chair. He does not drink or smoke because he has stomach ulcers, but Martin has grown very fond of him and asked him to write a short autobiography which he will use in his book.

While we were sat with George a very pious old woman, whom we see regularly going about her business, came up to us to tell us that she was worried because her employer had asked her to go to work at 6am the next day. This was too early for the first bus, so George, speaking in his best Byzantine Greek advised her to go home, kneel in front of her bed, put her hands together in prayer, and say to God: 'Dear God, who created the fleas to benefit mankind with their warm and nourishing milk, send me Nathaniel's Wings to carry me over to my Englishwoman master.' As I translated the prayer for Martin the old woman walked away cursing George for his blasphemy.

George and Xenou are very old friends and one can see their sympathy for each other is a very deep. But there are arguments as well, especially about prices. Xenou is very forgetful and tends to mix the prices of her goods up. George on the other hand, despite being a communist, is very money conscious and very good at sums. The argument this time was about how much George owed Xenou. George said it was 3/6 and explained why. Xenou insisted it was 3/8 and proceeded to tell him an Aesopian tale about a stubborn peasant like himself.

Her story went like this: 'A peasant was walking to his field with his wife when, somewhere ahead of them, they saw what looked like a group of animals sitting under a tree. The peasant said to his wife, "Look at those stray sheep, I wonder who they belong to." The wife replied, "They are not sheep. Can't you see their wings and that they are walking on two legs?" In going a little closer some of the creatures flapped their wings and flew away. "There, you see!" said the wife. "They are not sheep, they are birds because they fly." But the peasant just replied, "I can see they can fly, but I tell you they are still sheep."'

28th August 1968: We all went to Kyrenia by bus for the day. We took the long way round, via Nicosia, because the short way has been closed by the Turks. This was everybody's first visit to the celebrated little town. Before we set off I made up my mind not to like it, and I didn't. But neither did the rest of our company.

Passing outside the Dome Hotel Martin remembered Roy Jenkins and went in to see him. Unfortunately Jenkins had left the day before. At least that is what the manager told him, but perhaps he thought Martin was an assassin with his bruised face, dark glasses and breath reminiscent decomposed pickled peppers.

Martin was already drunk by this time having spent the journey drinking from a small bottle of brandy. As we walked from the hotel towards the beach Martin fell down, hurting himself again, and had to be helped to his feet. Later, as we waited for the bus to take us home, Martin caused great offence to the other passengers by urinating against a wall in the open-air bus station.

31st August 1968: Within one day I recognised in the street two government ministers and the chairman of the state broadcasting authority, and I managed to secure a promise to be taken to see the President of Cyprus as soon as he returns from abroad. That is how small Cyprus is, and people are still very familiar with those in power. While I talked to the Minister of Commerce and Industry a man passing by patted him on the shoulder and said he would buy him a beer next time he is in town.

At home we received two letters from John, a friend in Leeds, saying he will be arriving in Cyprus on Monday and staying with us for eight days. One was posted in Glasgow and the other in Beirut. This created some panic because this particular friend is a very indiscreet homosexual and a noisy drinker.

When he drinks he sings a repertoire of Communist, obscene and religious songs which are bound to contravene the laws on blasphemy or at least upset the locals. In Leeds he also has the habit of taking round to Martin's place every young man he picks up in the local pubs. If he does the same thing here, in this suspicious and nosy neighbourhood, then God help us!

1st September 1968: Christine and I had some wicked thoughts about John's arrival. Could we let him eat unwashed peaches sprayed with insecticides, or perhaps just give him a dose of mild poison that might incapacitate him for eight days?

At the very least, Christine suggested, we should book him into the most expensive hotel in town so he might run out of money and leave early.

The best suggestion was to manufacture mysterious documents in Greek, plant them on him, and then send him into the Turkish quarter in the hope he might be arrested as a spy.

2nd September 1968: John arrived late in the afternoon. Martin and I went with him to St Lazarus Square in the old part of Larnaca, where we booked him a room at 7/- a night. Then we sat on the veranda of a restaurant facing the church of St Lazarus and had dinner and drinks. Martin and John ate with their fingers and sung *The Internationale* and *The Red Flag* several times.

Halfway through dinner John saw some youths in a coffeehouse across the street playing one of those abominable games on an electrified table and went to join them. I feared he was about to create an incident by some indecent suggestion. St Lazarus is an area frequented mostly by peasants from the surrounding villages who have very strong views against homosexuality.

The hypocrisy of Cypriots towards sex is extraordinary. There is an apparent attitude of protectiveness towards the female members of the family but this results in a lack of basic human rights for women, while young men are forgiven and allowed everything they can get away with, except of course any hint of homosexuality. I remember that before prostitution was outlawed in Cyprus teenage boys from the villages would save their money until they had 5/-. Then they would catch the village bus to St Lazarus Square from where they would run an early-morning and indiscreet race to the brothel in Water Street, much to the disgust of the townspeople.

In Water Street they all queued noisily to have sex with the same woman, before returning to the village chewing bunches of parsley which was believed ward-off VD.

6th September 1968: Martin, John and I went to Nicosia to collect a selection of poems Mr Panos Joannides had promised us for Martin's book. Mr Joannides is a Cypriot poet and high official in the broadcasting authority. We were offered drinks – beer and brandy – in his office before an English speaking technician was found to show us around the studios. John touched every switch in sight, so I wondered whether Cyprus would be left without television that night. He also took a liking to a man described as the 'hole maker', which for some reason meant he wrote the subtitles in Greek for foreign films.

Later, at the bus station, Martin was shaking badly and needed assistance to get down the three steps from the bus to the street. We got him a large brandy at a cafe nearby and this seemed to help. With Martin now in a better state we visited the Ministry of Education where we met our friends Pefkios and Panayiotis Serghis, and were given poems by the Minister's private secretary. Pefkios and Panayiotis took us to lunch in a place full of songbirds in cages. I remembered the last time I ate here one of the cages contained a large black snake.

Over lunch Pefkios asked John questions about his life, and John mentioned that he had been a scoutmaster.

Pefkios recalled the story Martin had told him on our visit to the mountains about knowing a scoutmaster who was a homosexual. Martin pretended not to know anything about the story, but he had told it and it was obvious to everyone that it was about John.

As we said our goodbyes Panayiotis said he'd try to arrange for Martin and me to see the President.

Before heading back to Larnaca we stopped to have a few expensive drinks at the People's Bar in Nicosia. A dissatisfied Martin declared, 'The People's Bar is deepest pink, it's not as red as people think.'

7th September 1968: The comments of some of our neighbours in Larnaca have not always being kind. At Xenou's a woman said, 'I did not see her clean her house in two months,' about Christine. 'And you can smell ouzo when you pass by on the street.' Another neighbour stopped me in the bank and said, 'Your wife allows the children to wander anywhere they like. I suppose that's how Englishwomen bring up their children.'

It is not only the neighbours. When I had my exhibition a newspaper said, 'With Mr Paraskos is Mr Martin Bell, a poet who is writing a book Cyprus, going around the streets dressed like a tramp even though he is said to be a university lecturer – a sign of our times!' We are regularly criticised for being the beatniks of Cyprus.

Mary and I took the family to Famagusta. When we returned our landlady said there was a message for me from the President's Palace at Xenou's. At Xenou's I met another neighbour, a woman who never so much as said good morning before. This time she smiled at me and said somebody from the government was trying to get in touch with me. 'She must think you're being deported,' Xenou said loudly. Then with equal volume so the whole shop could hear she told me that my friend from the Ministry of Education had rung up to say that President Makarios will see Martin and me on Monday at 11am.

That'll teach them who is a beatnik and who is a VIP!

Appendix B

Interview with Stass Paraskos, from a video recorded by King Adz in Lempa, Cyprus, summer 2006

Available on YouTube at:
www.youtube.com/watch?v=6HB2OK4pslo

This is the entrance to the College of Art in Lempa. The Great Wall of Lempa, as this entrance is called, it started in an accidental way. Originally, there was no wall separating the street from our yard, and we thought we'd build a wall. So we started building a low wall.

Some of the material we used for the wall was debris left behind by students. It was a works of art – they were works of art rejected by the students who'd finished their studies and went away. And we had a problem storing it.

Anyway, we put these materials on the wall. And of course, being artists, you're always an artist, even when you build a wall. So we did not just place items on top of each other together. We started arranging things. And when you start arranging, you notice visual rhythms going on between items. And one thing led to another. What was originally meant to be a wall started becoming a work of art.

What you see around here, is a major work of art, and somebody will appreciate it at some stage, although it's not finished yet, and we probably will never finish, but even as it is unfinished, it's got quality, and it counts as a major work of art. It's certainly the biggest public sculpture in Cyprus. You know, I thought we'd keep doing this in an open-ended way. And when we fill the yard, then we fill the studios as well and we go to the roof of the building so that the college of art becomes a work of art. You know, that was my intention at some way through. So I don't know if we'll ever managed to do that, but it's a good idea. It's a romantic way to finish a college of art, you know, to transform it into a work of art.

    When I was in England, nobody took much notice of me, except like, you know, in the 1960s, because of that court trial – there was a court case involving my work. And there was an interest then, and then I was forgotten totally. But at that time, I started getting jobs in colleges of art, and being a real peasant, I thought that was the important thing. I thought I couldn't deny myself the glory of teaching in a university, for example, because I only did primary school education. So it meant a lot to me, to be a college professor. And I kind of neglected art. Well, I kept working, I never stopped working, but I stopped having exhibitions, you know, I didn't bother.

Index

A
Abolition of centre/periphery binary – 18, 20, 83–86, 132, 200–202
Adalı, Kutlu – 44
Africa – 83
Agency – 16, 55, 64–65, 74–75, 86, 167, 185, 189, 199–200
AKEL (Cyprus communist party) – 126
Anaphotia – 52, 153
Anti-colonial critique – 7–9, 15, 53–54, 83–85, 127, 173–174, 187–188, 193, 200–202
Araeen, Rasheed – 79–80, 82–84, 184–187, 189, 197, 200–202
Art Bulletin (journal) – 64, 84, 187
Arts Council of Great Britain – 117, 154, 157, 160, 210, 212, 219
Aspetti, Tiziano – 41, 43
Atkinson, Eric "Ricky" – 120
Authenticity (folkloric trap) – 20, 64, 79–80, 84–85, 183–203

B
Bacon, Francis – 42
Bachelard, Gaston – 24, 38–40, 49
Bell, Martin – 14, 153–154, 159–161, 163, 165, 168–169, 172, 175–176, 204–223
Biennale, São Paulo – 83–85
Bourriaud, Nicolas – 145, 147–148, 165–166
Brah, Avtar – 45, 55, 69–74
Bracha Ettinger – 47
British colonialism – 7–9, 53–54, 120–121, 126–127, 137, 174, 176
British Home Office – 212
Britishness – 75

C
Canon formation – 18–20, 64, 79–80, 83–85, 122–123, 130–132, 175–176, 178–179, 185–186, 198, 201, 203
Canonical silencing – 18, 122, 130–132

Cattaneo, Danese – 41, 43
Censorship – 59, 73, 78, 87–133, 212
Centre/periphery – 7–9, 14–16, 18, 20, 64, 83–86, 132, 189–190, 195, 197, 200–202
Charnley, James – 120–122, 124, 127, 129–130
Chlorakas – 138
Christian, Barbara T. – 130–131
Christianity – 34, 56, 68
Colonial mimicry – 8–9, 176–177, 180–181, 199
Colonial narrative frameworks – 7–9, 53–54, 61–63, 120–121, 126–127, 129–133, 173–174, 200–202
Community networks (Cypriot diaspora) – 56–57, 60–63, 69–70, 76–77
Conceptual art – 12, 14–15, 19–20, 124, 129, 146–147, 178–180, 197–198
Constantinides, Pamela – 59, 76–77
Constructed identity – 55, 63–65, 74–75, 84–85, 164–169, 172–177, 181–182
Contemporary Art from Cyprus (book) – 177–180
Corridor8 – 81, 122, 127, 182
Creolisation – 70–73
Crump, Maurice – 88, 92–94, 98–99, 101, 116
Cultural hybridity – 82–86, 196–198, 201–202
Cultural memory – 24, 26, 31, 34–40, 49–51, 85
Cypriot community in London – 56–57, 60–63, 69, 76–77
Cypriot folklore – 24–25, 37, 40–41, 183–184, 188–189, 196–199, 201
Cyprus College of Art – 13–17, 19–20, 132–135, 138–144, 146–148, 150–153, 155–158, 164, 172–174, 176–177, 179–182, 190–192, 194, 196–197

D

Deena, Seodial – 130–131
Destiny (teleological framing) – 159, 165–168
Destruction in Art Symposium (DIAS) – 14

Dine, Jim – 97, 104, 114, 118–119
Dome Hotel, Kyrenia – 170, 211
Douthwaite, Pat – 78
Driberg, Tom – 212
Durrell, Lawrence – 120–121
Dury, Ian – 78

E

Ecofeminism – 41–42
Eleni Nikita – 11, 83, 183–184, 188, 198–200
Emplotment – 6–8, 16, 61–62, 127, 130–132, 134–136, 150, 163–164
EOKA – 126–127
Essentialism – 6, 18, 50, 85, 188–189, 199, 202
Ethnic artist label – 79–80, 185–186, 197, 200–201
Ethnographic gaze – 79–80, 175, 186–188, 200
Exile – 36, 38–40, 49–51

F

Famagusta – 138
Feminised landscape – 24, 40–44, 49–50
Feminist critique – 24, 41–44, 49–50, 132
Fluxus – 14, 124, 146
Folkloric inflection – 188, 202
Folkloric trap – 79–80, 123, 182–203
Folklore – 24–25, 36–37, 40–41, 183–184, 188–189, 196–199, 201
Fantasy and Figuration (exhibition) – 78
Frost, Terry – 80

G

Gaze, male – 42–44, 50
Gaze, Western – 15–16, 79, 82, 84–85, 132–133, 176, 185, 188–189, 195–196, 202
Gendering of land – 24, 40–44, 49–50
Genius loci – 37–39

Geography as identity – 24, 31, 35–37, 49–51, 83–84
Giorgione (*The Sleeping Venus*) – 41, 43–44
Gombrich, Ernst – 29–31, 33–34
Great Wall of Lempa – 13–14, 16–17, 132–154, 179–180, 192, 196–197
Green Line (Cyprus) – 136, 192–193
Gropius, Walter – 134
Guardian, The (newspaper) – 9–10, 13, 59, 69, 90, 100–102, 104–105, 108–110, 114–115, 118, 182–184

H

Hall, Stuart – 45, 55, 75, 79, 84–85
Hegemony – 75–76, 79–80, 84–85, 132, 195, 198
Hellbeck, Jochen – 159–160, 164–165
Hermeneutic silencing – 18, 122, 130–132
Heterogeneity (diasporic identity) – 70–71, 83–85, 200–202
Horton, Derek – 81–82, 122–123, 127–129, 182–183
Hybridity – 82–86, 196–198, 201–202
Happening / Happenings – 14, 146
Harwood, Ronald – 116
Hetherington, John – 92–93
Hilton Hotel (Nicosia) – 154, 205–206, 208, 213, 215
Huddersfield Daily Examiner – 106
Hughes, Glyn – 178
Hughes, Patrick (Peter) – 59, 87, 104, 115

I

Identity – 15–16, 23, 55, 63–65, 74–75, 84–85, 166, 171, 181
Identity, Cypriot – 6, 52, 68–69, 75–76, 83–85, 188–189, 199
Identity, new ethnicities – 84–85
Identity, postcolonial – 8–9, 19, 53–54, 83–85, 154, 171–173, 180–181, 200–202
Innocent Eye, The (Herbert Read) – 32–33, 164–165
Institutions – 11–12, 18–20, 45, 132–133, 174, 177–178, 180–181, 186, 189, 194

Interiorised landscape – 24, 35, 39–40, 49–50
Invasion (Turkish, 1974) – 48, 56, 138, 169–170
Institute of Contemporary Arts (ICA) – 78, 119
Icons (Orthodox Christian) – 34

J

Jameson, Anna – 162
Jenkins, Roy – 115, 170, 211–212
Johnson, W. E. – 9, 119–120, 122, 182–183
Jones, John – 110
Jew, George Edward – 91, 97, 98, 101

K

Kazantzakis, Nikos – 46
Kissonerga (village) – 138
Kitchen, Herbert – 78
Knowledge production – 18, 64, 79, 83, 122, 132–133, 176, 185–186, 188, 195–196, 202
Kyrenia – 165, 170, 211

L

Landscape, allegorical – 24, 28–31, 34, 49–51
Landscape, Cypriot modern – 36, 45–46, 49–50, 140
Landscape, feminised – 24, 40–44, 49–50
Landscape, remembered – 24, 31, 36–40, 49–50
Landscape violence – 45–46, 48–50, 139–141
Leeds (city) – 9, 59, 66, 73, 78, 87, 103, 120, 122, 124, 127–128
Leeds College of Art – 13, 30, 59, 66–67, 87, 103, 109, 120–122, 124, 129
Lemba/Lempa (village) – 13, 15, 132, 137–141, 145, 151, 191
Locke, Hew – 198, 200–202
London Cypriot community – 56–57, 60–63, 69, 76–77
Lynton, Norbert – 78, 90, 98–100, 105, 107, 109, 114–118, 124–128, 132–134, 139–141, 151

Lady Chatterley's Lover (trial) – 95–96
Leicester Mercury – 99, 103, 114, 118, 154
Liminality – 139

M

Male gaze – 42–44, 50
Manifesta Organisation – 14–16, 82, 189–196
Marginalisation – 7, 10–12, 15, 64, 74, 79–82, 118–123, 127–133, 174–178, 182, 185–189, 194–196, 199–200
Marginality – 12, 18, 45, 52–55, 74, 83, 132, 139, 186–187
Matrixial zone – 47, 83, 165
Memory, cultural – 24, 26, 31, 34–40, 49–51, 85
Merchant, Carolyn – 24, 41–42, 49
Migration, economic – 52–55, 60–61
Migration, symbolic – 53–54, 63–65
Migrant labour – 54, 60, 62–63, 67–68
Mimicry – 8–9, 176–177, 180–181, 199
Mitter, Partha – 64, 84, 187
Mythic landscapes – 24–26, 28, 36–37, 49–51
Makarios, Archbishop President – 14, 154–155, 158, 166, 169–172, 175–176
Marcuse, Herbert – 144
McNay, M.G. – 10, 101
Metaxas, Stefos – 143, 146, 150
Mir, Salam – 172–173
Miró, Joan – 133, 151
Montgomerie Committee – 116

N

Naïve art – 5–7, 9–12, 64–65, 80–81, 119–120, 122–123, 128, 132–133, 182–185, 188–189, 199–200
National identity (Cypriot) – 83, 171–173, 175–176, 181–182
Nationhood – 8, 19, 53, 154, 169, 171–174, 181–182
Nicosia – 126, 136, 154–155, 165, 170, 190, 194, 204–206, 208, 212–

213, 215
Nitsch, Hermann – 118

O

Obscenity trial (Leeds, 1966) – 59, 73–75, 78–79, 87–133, 212
Orientalism – 15, 81, 120, 132–133, 186–189, 195–196, 202
Otherness – 64, 74, 79, 84, 185–186, 197, 200–202
Osborne, Charles – 160, 220–221
Ovenden, Graham – 78
Other Story, The (exhibition) – 185

P

Page, Robin – 14, 101, 123, 129, 146
Paraskos, Stass, arrival narrative – 60–63
Paraskos, Stass, as "naïve" – 5–7, 9–12, 64–65, 80–81, 119–120, 122–123, 128, 132–133, 182–185, 188–189, 199–200
Patriarchy – 24, 42–44, 49–50
Periphery – 7–9, 14–16, 18, 20, 64, 83–86, 132, 189–190, 195, 197, 200–202
Phenomenology of memory – 24, 35–40, 49–50
Poetics – 24, 38–40, 49–50
Postcolonial Cyprus – 8–9, 19, 53, 154, 170, 171–174, 176, 180–182
Postcolonial theory – 7–9, 19, 53, 83–85, 127, 176, 187–189, 195, 200–202
Primitivism – 10, 64, 119, 182, 186
Panofsky, Erwin – 29–30
Paperno, Irina – 162–165, 168, 170–172
Phelan, Peggy – 147–148, 151–152
Porter, Peter – 160, 221–223
Potter, Dennis – 100

R

Read, Herbert – 9, 24, 31–33, 38, 40, 104, 106–109, 120, 164–165
Rose, Gillian – 24, 42–44, 47, 49–50

Randolph, John Hugh Edward – 107, 113
Reichardt, Jasia – 117–118
Relational Aesthetics – 145, 147–148, 165–166

S

Said, Edward – 187–188, 201
São Paulo Biennale – 83–85
Sleeping Venus, The (Giorgione) – 43–44
Spectatorship – 42, 47, 50, 79, 82, 84, 176, 185, 188, 195
Susanna and the Elders (Gentileschi) – 47
Savva, Christoforos – 178–179
Selnsucht – 24
Shabout, Nada – 173–174
Space and Place – 35, 37
Stone, Bob – 142
Stylianou, Elena – 177–178
Swearing – 84–85

T

Tetley, The (Leeds art gallery) – 81, 121–122, 127
Topophilia – 24, 36–37, 49
Tradition – 5, 18–20, 70–72, 85, 198, 201
Trayte, Jonathan – 81, 122, 127, 182
Turkish invasion of Cyprus (1974) – 48, 56, 138, 169–170
Taylor, Eric – 59, 87, 103, 109, 115, 124
Thubron, Harry – 12, 66–67, 71, 124
Titian – 41, 43–44
Toumazis, Yiannis – 178, 190
Tuan, Yi-Fu – 24, 34–38, 49
Tselika, Evanthia – 177–178

U

University art departments (Cyprus) – 11–12, 177–178

Unmarked: The Politics of Performance – 147–148, 151–152
Utilitarianism – 149

V
Vagrancy Acts – 91–93, 99, 104–106, 108–109, 114–117, 212
van de Velde, Henry – 133–134
Vernis, Anthony – 220, 223
Votsis, Stelios – 143, 146, 150

W
Waldvogel, Florian – 193–194
Warren, Wilfred – 93–94
Waterman, Harry – 105
White, Hayden – 6–8, 61, 127–128, 134, 163
Whitehouse, Mary – 100
Wilson, Harold – 100
Windrush Generation – 54

Y
Yearning – 24, 36, 38, 40, 49–51

Z
Zorba the Greek (Nikos Kazantakis) – 10, 46

www.ingramcontent.com/pod-product-compliance
Lightning Source LLC
Chambersburg PA
CBHW011404210526
45464CB00010B/3038